John Thomas Bell

History of Washington County, Nebraska

its early settlement and present status, resources, advantages and future

prospects

John Thomas Bell

History of Washington County, Nebraska

its early settlement and present status, resources, advantages and future prospects

ISBN/EAN: 9783744741354

Printed in Europe, USA, Canada, Australia, Japan

Cover: Foto ©ninafisch / pixelio.de

More available books at **www.hansebooks.com**

NEBRASKA

Its Early Settlement and Present Status, Resources, Advantages and Future Prospects.

JOHN T. BELL, Law Reporter, Omaha, Neb.

OMAHA, NEB.
PRINTED AT THE HERALD STEAM BOOK AND JOB PRINTING HOUSE.
JULY, 1876.

THE COUNTY IN THE PAST.

FIRST SETTLEMENT IN 1819.—LEWIS AND CLARKE'S POW-WOW WITH THE INDIANS.—ORGANIZATION OF THE TERRITORY AND COUNTY.—LIST OF COUNTY OFFICIALS—NEWSPAPERS.—THE BIG STORM.

The first white settlement made in Nebraska was at a point now included within the boundaries of Washington county, on which the town of Fort Calhoun is located. It was here, also, that the first council was ever held by the whites with the Indians of the then unexplored northwest—a vast region of country extending from the Red river of the South to the British possessions, and from the Mississippi to the Pacific ocean.

In 1803 was consummated what is known as the Louisiana purchase, which included the present state of Nebraska, and the attention of the United States government was directed towards exploring and improving the newly acquired territory. Accordingly, in the summer of 1803, an expedition was planned by President Jefferson, for the purpose of discovering the course and sources of the Missouri, and the most convenient water communication thence to the Pacific. His private secretary, Capt. Merriweather Lewis, and Capt. William Clarke, both officers in the army, were detailed to undertake this enterprise. These two officers met at St. Louis in the month of December, intending to pass the winter at La Charrette, the highest settlement on the Missouri, but the Spanish commandant of the province, not having received official notification of the transfer of the province to the United States, refused to allow them to pass through. The party, therefore, encamped on the eastern bank of the Mississippi, which formed the eastern boundary of the Spanish possessions, opposite the mouth of the Missouri. The party was composed of nine young Kentuckians, fourteen soldiers, who had volunteered their services, two French *roygeurs*, an interpreter and hunter, and a colored servant belonging to Capt. Clarke ; all but the latter being enlisted as privates to serve during the expedition, three of their number being appointed sergeants. In addition a corporal, six soldiers, and nine *royageurs*, accompanied the expedition as far as the Mandan nation in order to assist in carrying the stores or repelling an Indian assault. The stores consisted of a great variety of clothing, tools, gunlock flints, powder and ball. To these were added fourteen bales and one box of goods designed as Indian presents, and consisting of richly laced coats, medals, flags, knives, tomahawks, beads, looking glasses, colored handkerchiefs, paint, etc. The party had three boats, one being a keel boat, fifty-five feet long, drawing three feet of water, and carrying one large square sail, and twenty-two oars. A deck of ten feet in the bow and stern formed a forecastle and cabin, while the middle was covered by lockers which could be raised so as to form breastworks in case of attack. The two other boats were open, one carrying six and the other seven oars. Two horses were at the same time to be led along the banks of the river for the purpose of bringing home game, or hunting, in case of scarcity.

Thus accoutered, the party started on its toilsome journey up the Missouri Monday, May 14th, 1804, and reached the mouth of the Platte July 21, encamping the next day "ten miles from the Platte, intending to make the requisite observations, and to send for the neighboring tribes for the purpose of making known the recent change in the government, and the wish of the United States to cultivate their friendship." July 27th the expedition proceeded up the river, and on the 30th reached the place where the council was to be held, having passed Boyer creek the day before. The country and the council are described as follows, in Lewis and Clarke's official report, for a copy of which I am indebted to Byron Reed, of Omaha:

"The land here consists of a plain, above the high water level, the soil of which is fertile and covered with a grass from five to eight feet high, interspersed with copses of large plums and a currant like those of the United States. It also furnishes two species of honeysuckle, one growing to a kind of a shrub, common about Harrodsburg, Kentucky, and the other not so high. The flowers grow in clusters, are short and of a light pink color. The leaves, too, are distinct, and do not surround the stem as do those of the United States. Back of this plain is a woody ridge about seventy feet above it, at the end of which we formed our camp. This ridge separates the lower from a higher prairie of a good quality, with grass of ten or twenty inches in height, and extending back about a mile to another elevation of eighty or ninety feet, beyond which is one continuous plain. Near our camp we enjoy from the bluffs a most beautiful view of the river and the adjoining country. At a distance varying from four to ten miles, and of a height between seventy and three hundred feet, two parallel ranges of high land afford a passage to the Missouri, which enriches the low grounds between them. In its winding course it nourishes the willow islands, the scattered cottonwood, elm, sycamore, lynn, and ash; and the groves are interspersed with hickory, walnut, coffeenut, and oak. The hunters supplied us with deer, turkeys, geese and beaver. Catfish are abundant in the river, and we have also seen a buffalo-fish. One of our men brought in yesterday an animal called by the Pawnees, chocantoosh, and by the French, blairvau, or badger.

"We waited with much anxiety the return of our messenger to the Ottoes. Our apprehensions were at last relieved by the arrival of a party of about fourteen Ottoe and Missouri Indians, who came at sunset on the second of August, accompanied by a Frenchman who resided among them and interpreted for us. Captains Lewis and Clarke went out to meet them and told them that we would hold a council in the morning. In the meantime we sent them some roasted meats, pork, flour and meal in return for which they made us a present of watermelons.

"The next morning, the Indians, with their six chiefs were all assembled under an awning formed with the mainsail, in the presence of all of our party, paraded for the occasion. A speech was then made announcing to them the change in the government, our promises of protection, and advice as to their future conduct. All the six chiefs replied to our speech, each in his turn according to rank. They expressed their joy at the change in the government, their hopes that we would recommend them to their great father (the president) that they might obtain trade and necessaries. They wanted arms as well for hunting as for defence and asked our mediation between them and the Mahas (Omahas) with whom they are now at war. We promised to do so and wished some of them to accompany us to that nation which they declined, for fear of being killed by them. We then proceeded to distribute our presents. The grand chief of the nation not being of the party we sent him a flag, a medal and some ornaments for clothing. To the six chiefs who were present we gave a medal of the second grade to one Ottoe chief and a Missouri chief and a medal of the third grade to two inferior chiefs of each nation, the customary mode of recognizing a chief being to place a medal around his neck, which is considered among his tribe a proof of his consideration abroad. Each of these medals was accompanied by a present of paint, garters and cloth ornaments of dress, and to this we added a cannister of powder, a bottle of whisky and a few presents to the whole, which appeared to make them perfectly satisfied. The air gun, too, was fired and astonished them greatly. The absent grand chief was an Ottoe named Wahrushhah which, in English, degenerates into Little Thief. The two principal chieftans present were Shongolongo, or Big Horse and Wethea, or Hospitality; also Shosquscan, or White Horse, an Ottoe. The incidents just related induced us to give to this place the name of Council-bluff. The situation of it is exceedingly favorable for a fort and trading factory, as the soil is well calculated for bricks and there is an abundance of wood in the neighborhood, and the air being pure and healthy. It is also central to the chief resorts of the Indians, being one day's journey to the Ottoes; one and a half to the great Pawnees; two days from the Mahas; two and a quarter from the Pawnee Loups village; convenient to the hunting grounds of the Sioux, and twenty-five days journey to Sante Fe. The ceremonies of the council being concluded, we set sail in the afternoon and encamped at the distance of five miles on the south side, where we found the musquitos very troublesome." And, to tell the truth, they are very troublesome in that vicinity to this day, at certain seasons of the year.

Though the early settlers of Council Bluffs, Iowa, have endeavored to make it appear that their town is located upon the site of this olden time conference, the fact is established beyond all question that they were in error and that the site of the present town of Fort Calhoun, is the exact locality. At this point the government established Fort Atkinson—afterwards called Fort Calhoun—in 1819, and abandoned it some ten or a dozen years later. In response to a letter of inquiry on this subject from Mr. N. Ramsey, secretary of the Historical society of St. Louis, under date of December 9, 1867, the late Father De Smet wrote: " During the years 1838 and 1839, I resided opposite what is now called the city of Omaha. In 1839 I stood on the bluff on which the old fort was built in 1819; some rubbish and remains of the old Foot were then visible, and some remaining roots of asparagus were still growing in the old garden. Fort Atkinson was located where now stands the town of Fort Calhoun, Nebraska Territory, about sixteen miles in a straight line above the city of Omaha, and forty miles by river. The mouth of the Boyer now empties into the Missouri river, some twelve miles (straight line) above Omaha: in 1839 the same river emptied into the Missouri river about five miles above the old military post. Mr. Cabanne's trading post was six miles, by land, below Fort Atkinson, and twenty-five miles by river; Mr. Cabanne's trading post was ten miles, by land, above where now stands Omaha City. Manual Lisa had a trading post one mile above Cabanne's. I met Captains Joseph and John La Barge, and proposed the question of the former site of Fort Atkinson, in order to test the accuracy of my memory, and they confirmed it in every particular."

On the 30th of May, 1854. the organicact, opening Kansas and Nebraska for settlement, was passed by Congress. Francis Burt of South Carolina was appointed Governor of Nebraska, but was taken sick while on his way to the new territory and died soon after his arrival, at the old Mission House at Bellevue on the 18th day of October, 1853. By the death of Governor Burt, the Secretary of the Territory, Thos. B. Cuming, became acting Governor, and his first official action was certain proclamations: One ordering a census of the Territory upon which to base an apportionment; another fixing the time of holding the election, and convening the legislature; and one dividing the Territory into counties and fixing boundaries to the same. By the terms of the latter Washington county was bounded as follows: Commencing at a point on the Missouri river one mile north of Omaha city; thence due west to the dividing ridge between the Elkhorn and the Missouri river; thence northwestwardly twenty miles to the Elkhorn river; thence eastwardly to a point on the Missouri river two miles above Fort Calhoun; thence southerly along said river to the place of beginning.

The Territory was divided by Gov. Cuming into four election districts with voting places distributed as folows: Bellvue, Omaha, Fontenelle, and Fort Calhoun. Dr. M. H. Clark and Col. Wm. Kline laid out the Fontenelle or Western district, which extended from the big Papillion to Fort Kearney, or, in fact, to the Rocky Mountains. There is a tradition in the western part of the county to the effect that, in order to swell the list of voters, these enterprising individuals included in their census returns a lot of names copied from the trees at the crossing of the Elkhorn, where they had been carved by California and Mormon emigrants, but this may be a base slander.

The counties were not named by the Governor, but were christened by the first legislature, which met at Omaha in the winter of 1854-5, and consisted of eight Councilmen—four from each side of the Platte—and thirteen Representatives, Washington county sending, as Councilman James G. Mitchell, and as Representatives, Anselum Arnold, and A. J. Smith. February 22, 1855, an act was passed declaring that "a county shall be organized to be called Washington, and shall be bounded as follows: Commencing at a point on the Missouri river, two miles north of Florence, or Winter Quarters, thence north following the meanderings of said river to a point in a direct line, twenty-four miles from the place of beginning, thence west to the dividing ridge between the Elkhorn and Missouri rivers, or to the eastern boundary line of Dodge county, thence south along said line twenty-four miles, thence east to the place of beginning." Fort Calhoun was designated as the county seat, and the following were appointed county officers, by the Governor: Stephen Cass, Probate Judge; Thomas Allen, Sheriff; Geo. W. Nevelle, Clerk; George Martin, Treasurer; Z. Jackson, Register, and Thos. Wilson, Surveyor. Since that date the following named have been elected to the various positions designated:

COUNCILMEN—Wm. Clancy, 1856; G. E. Scott, and Geo. W. Doane (now of Omaha), floater, 1858; John A. Unthank, 1860; E. A. Allen and Frank Welch, of Burt, floater, 1862; John D. Neighley, of Cuming, floater, 1866.

STATE SENATORS—Jesse T. Davis, 1866; W. F. Goodwill, of Burt, floater, 1868; B. F. Hilton, 1870; L. W. Osborn, 1872; Waldo Lyon, of Burt, floater, 1874.

REPRESENTATIVES—Wm. Connor, Elisha P. Stout, and James S. Stewart, 1856; P. C. Sullivan, R. H. Peterson, and James S. Stewart, 1857; P. G. Cooper, L. M. Kline, and Charles Davis, 1858; James S. Stewart, and John S. Bowen, 1859; Silas Mead, and Henry W. De Pugh, 1860; E. A. Allen, and John S. Bowen, 1861; L. R. Fletcher, and Dean C. Slader, 1862. [The session of the legislature for the winter of 1862-3 was dispensed with by act of congress, and the money, equal to the expense of the session applied to war purposes.] John Evans (now of Omaha), and H. J. Rohwer, 1863; H. M. Hitchcock, and Nevin McCandlish, 1864; E. H. Clark, and Charles Eisley, 1865; A. S. Warrick, and Dr. L. J. Abbott, Territorial, and John A. Unthank, and Dean C. Slader, State Representatives, 1866—there being two sets elected on account of a State constitution having been drafted; W. H. B. Stout (now contractor for the erection of the State's prison), and Christian Rathmann, 1868; Elam Clark, and H. C. Riordan, 1870; Henry Sprick, 1872—a new apportionment having given the county but one member of the House—E. S. Gaylord, 1874.

In July, 1866, a special session of the legislature was held, in which Frank Welch, of Burt, represented Washington county as Senator, and

Wm. R. Hamilton, D. McDonald, and Thomas R. Wilson as Representatives.

COMMISSIONERS—David Franklin, A. Phinney, and John West, 1856; J. B. Wickwire, 1857; E. Allen, 1858; E. B. Hamilton, 1859; John Parks, 1860; John Evans, and James S. Stewart (the latter to fill Mr. Parks' unexpired term), 1861; Silas Masters, 1862; Jacob Carter, 1863; Jas. S. Stewart, re-elected 1864; John A. Unthank (appointed to fill the unexpired term of Silas Masters, resigned), 1865; W. B. Beals, 1866; Alonzo Perkins, 1867; Thos. Frazier, 1868; Watson Tyson, 1869; Wm. R. Hamilton, and David Couchman (the latter to fill the unexpired term of Thos. Frazier, deceased), 1870; David Couchman. re-elected 1871; Watson Tyson, re-elected 1872; Wm. R. Hamilton, re-eletced 1873; H. J. Rohwer, 1874; Charles Selleck, 1875,

COUNTY CLERKS—E. Mather, 1857; Abram Castetter, 1861; re-elected every election from that time to 1869, when Peter R. Benner was elected and re-elected in 1871 and 1873; E. C. Jackson, 1875.

COUNTY TREASURERS—George Stevens, 1857, Lewis Tucker, 1858; E. N. Grennell, 1859; re-elected each election until 1863, when Alex Reed was elected, and he was continued in office until 1875, when J. H. Hungate, the present incumbent and the then Mayor of Blair, was elected.

SHERIFFS—Orrin Rhodes, and Hugh McNeely (the latter to fill unexpired term), 1856; Hugh McNeeley, 1857; Chester Lusk, 1860; Israel Swihart, 1861, Dan Case, 1868; A. T. Chapin, 1869; Rice Arnold, 1871, and re-elected in 1873 and 1875.

PROBATE JUDGES—James A. Goodrich, 1757; Z. Jackson, 1861; John S. Bowen, 1869, and re-elected in 1871; Jesse T. Davis, 1873, and re-elected in 1875.

SUPERINTENDENTS OF SCHOOLS—Eli Bacon, 1857; D. McLacklin, 1858; Charles G. Bisbee, 1869; re-elected in 1871; Charles Cross, 1873; re elected in 1875.

SURVEYORS—Thomas Wilson, 1857; re-elected in 1858; George Brigham, 1861; V. G. Lantry, 1869; re-elected in 1871; J. C. W. Kline, 1875,

CORONERS—Jesse T. Davis, 1861; Charles Emerson Tennant, 1869; H. P. Butler 1871; Dr. S. B. Taylor, 1873; E. C. Pierce, 1875.

Mr. Ballard represented Washington county in the constitutional convention of 1871, and E. N. Grennell and J. J. Thompson in that of 1875.

The foregoing list of officers is incomplete, but is a full as can be made after a thorough overhauling of the county records.

In the vote upon the constitution, submitted in 1871, Washington county cast 94 for and 419 votes against the section, submitted separately, granting women the right of suffrage, and 194 for to 319 against the compulsory education clause, also submitted separately, while she rejected the constitution itself by a majority of 97 votes. At the special election held in 1868, on the proposition to aid the construction of the Sioux City and Pacific railroad by voting county bonds to the amount of $75,000, to be paid only so fast as a tax of one mill on the dollar would pay it, the vote stood 347 for to 153 against the issuance of the bonds.

The following named have occupied the position of Deputy County Clerk, an office conferred by appointment: Roger T. Beal, D. McDonald Peter R. Benner, E. B. Hamilton, John S. Bowen, Harry M. Bowen, and Cara Clark, the present incumbent. Treasurer Hungate's deputy, is also a lady—Miss Edna Reed.

At the first election held in the county, in 1855, there were 70 votes polled. At the last general election—that of 1875—there were 1,180 ballots cast. The first census returns showed a population of 207; that of last year, 6,286, there being 314 births in the county in 1875. The following has been the annual levy since 1859:

For the year	1859			$ 7,555 25
"	"	"	'60	6,569 24
"	"	"	'61	7,284 02
"	"	"	'62	7,763 91
"	"	"	'63	9,642 61
"	"	"	'64	12,382 65
"	"	"	'65	16,035 10
"	"	"	'66	17,690 01
"	"	"	'67	24,583 90
"	"	"	'68	28,401 80
"	"	"	'69	42,389 73
"	"	"	'70	67,593 28
"	"	"	'71	86,542 30
"	"	"	'72	64,817 62
"	"	"	'73	86,782 56
"	"	"	'74	77,631 81
"	"	"	'75 (about)	86,000 00

The assessed valuation of property for this year was $1,551,756, with $75,000 exemption on account of the planting of trees, the exemption being at the rate of the tax, and on fifty dollars for each acre of fruit trees on one hundred dollars valuation for each acre of forest trees, for the term of five years after the trees were planted. This was one of the wisest acts ever performed by any legislature, and the result will be that in the course of a few years Nebraska will be a well timbered state. The law is generally appreciated and acted upon by the people, Sheridan precinct alone receiving an exemption for 1875 of $23,000 on account of tree planting, while Grant and Lincoln was each benefitted about $10,000.

The first newspaper published in the county was the DeSota *Bugle*, established at DeSoto in 1856 by Isaac Parrish; the second was the DeSoto *Pilot*, established in 1857 by Merrick & Maguire; the third the Washington county *Sun*, established in 1858 by Potter C. Sullivan, and the fourth was the DeSoto *Enquirer*, established in 1858 by Z. Jackson. Then there was a lull in the newspaper publishing business, until 1869, when the *Register* was established at Blair, by B. F. Hilton & Son. In 1870 the publication of the Blair *Times* was undertaken by a company consisting of C. B. Herman, John S. Bowen, J. H. Post, V. G. Lantry, H. P. Dexter, Jesse

T. Davis, Abram Castetter, Alex. Reed, W. H. B. Stout, and W. W. Wilson. In a few months it passed into the hands of V. G. Lantry. and W. H. B. Stout, then into the hands of the former, who sold it to John A. McMurphy, now editor and proprietor of the Plattsmouth *Herald*. Mr. McMurphy conducted the paper for a year or two, and then sold it back to Mr. Lantry, who sold it last spring to Judge John S. Bowen, by whom it is now managed in a very able manner. Two years ago J. Y. Lambert, editor and proprietor of the *Pilot*, published at Tekamah, Burt county, moved that paper to Blair, and there published it until about a year ago, when it was purchased by George Sultherland. It is now edited by L. F. Hilton, formerly of the *Register*, and is one of the spiciest, most enterprising weeklies in the State.

The winters of 1856-7 found the settlers of Washington county little prepared for its hardships. The winters of 1855-6 had been remarkably pleasant and mild, and it was supposed by the few white residents of the county at that time that that was a fair sample of the Nebraska winters. The houses were generally of a temporary character, many of them having been built the summer previous of new cottonwood lumber, which material makes beautiful "open work" after a few days exposure to the sun, rendering a building cool and airy for summer use, but not so pleasant for winter. Little or no shelter had been prepared for stock, and as there was a dearth of feed, cattle were allowed to wander here and there through the small patches of breaking, finding an occasional stray stalk of sod corn with which to astonish their stomachs. No one was provided with wood for more than a few days' use. Provisions were very scarce, and money scarcer. Such was the condition of things when the sun went down on the evening of the 30th of November, 1856. A light snow was falling, and had been for an hour, but the air was mild and pleasant, with a light wind. During the night the wind increased to a terrific gale; the weather grew intensely cold, and the air was filled with the driving snow, which was forced into the houses through a thousand and one crevices, covering beds, chairs, tables, stoves, etc., with a cold mantle of white. The day dragged by, with the wind surging and roaring and the air so thick with cutting, blinding snow that one could not see a house five feet distant; thus rendering it impossible for the stock to be fed, as a man could not find his way back to the house after leaving it. Several made the attempt, and perished in consequence, their bones being found when the snow melted the next spring, in some instances, within a short distance of their homes. Night settled upon us cold and dreary, and another day of suffering dawned and passed without the least prospect of relief. A second night and third day passed by, during which the wind seemed to have lost none of its fury, while the snow appeared to come from some inexhaustable source, whirling, eddying and driving, piling and drifting in the houses to a depth of two or three feet. As the evening of the third day came on, the anxious settlers were rejoiced to find that the storm was gradually losing its force. Another miserable night passed, and the fourth day dawned. The wind had gone down, and the sun rose bright and clear upon a brilliant, glistening, dazzling sea of snow, streching away as far as the vision extended, covering the ground to a depth of three or four feet on the level, while in the ravines it was drifted in places to the depth of twenty feet. The writer remembers distinctly of finding snow in a sheltered nook, the next June. The storm having subsided the settlers turned out to take care of their stock. In many places stables were built down in ravines, and were so completely covered with snow that some time elapsed before they could be found and the horses they sheltered—and very effectually too—dug out. Great difficulty was also experienced in gathering together the roaming cattle, and many perished in the storm.

THE PAWNEE WAR.

MILITARY ARDOR AT FEVER HEAT.—ON THE TRAIL.—A FAITHFUL SQUAW.—THE CAPTURE AND THE RESULT.

In the summer of 1859 occurred what has since passed into the realms of history as the "Pawnee war." Fontenelle was no longer the frontier settlement. Thirty miles to the northwest, on the Elkhorn, the town of West Point had been located, and six miles beyond, that of DeWitt. Ten miles southward, on the Platte, Fremont had been staked out two summers previous, while farther to the westward, along the Platte, were the new towns of North Bend and Columbus. The Pawnee Indians then occupied two villages about twelve miles directly south of Fontenelle, and on the south side of the Platte. They had behaved themselves very well, considering, their depredations having consisted mainly in robbing hen roosts and picking up little odds and ends of personal effects belonging to the whites, and the settlers had concluded there was no danger whatever to be apprehended from them, but in this they were doomed to disappointment.

In the latter part of June, 1859, the entire tribe of Pawnees—braves, squaws, pappooses and dogs—left their villages and marched across the low land intervening between the Platte and the Elkhorn rivers, and camp on the Elkhorn on the western side of that stream just across from Fontanelle. Here they remained a day or two; after which short delay, they proceeded up the Elkhorn, without crossing it, pursuing a northwesterly direction. They said they were going up the river on a grand buffalo hunt, and would be gone several "moons." On the day after they left their first camp on the Elkhorn, half a dozen "bucks" crossed the river at a point about a dozen miles above Fontenelle, and attacked an old bachelor by the name of Uriah Thomas, who was living alone in a little log hut some distance from any other house. The Indians took his pocketbook, containing $136, a package of valuable papers, including several land warrants, drank up all his whisky (the unkindest cut of all) and then drove off a fine yoke of oxen, after first having taken the precaution to lock Mr. Thomas up in his shanty. After the Indians had been gone for some time, Thomas set about effecting his release, which he accomplished with but little difficulty, and then cautiously proceeded to

Fontenelle and gave the alarm. Of course, the wildest excitement prevailed. A company of a dozen men or so was immediately organized, and an advance was made upon the Thomas mansion, after a careful reconoitering by scouts. No Indians were discovered, and the party concealed themselves in and about the hut, and waited patiently for several hours ; but no Indians making their appearance, the whites returned to Fontenelle. Two days afterwards, the people living at West Point and DeWitt (the settlements spoken of as being farther up the Elkhorn),came down to Fontenelle in a body, and reported that as the Pawnees moved up the river, on the western side of it, marauding bands had crossed over to the eastern side, and had burned the dwellings of the settlers, ripped up their feather beds, scattered the contents, and used the ticks for blankets ; tore to pieces clocks for the purpose of getting the brass wheels to hang in their ears and drove off all kinds of stock.

This was a fine state of affairs. Thirty men, armed with rifles, shotguns, muskets, and revolvers, started for West Point the next morning in wagons, reaching that settlement about the middle of the afternoon. They saw no Indians that day, and after deliberating over the matter, concluded to return to Fontenelle the next day. As they were on the point of starting, a scout came in with the information that he had seen a small body of Indians crossing the river a mile or so distant. Arrangements were instantly made to capture the party. A portion of the white men took position in one room of a double log house, while the rest of the party kept themselves out of sight. The people of the house were instructed to admit the Indians into the unoccupied room of the house, and after they were all in the room, the outside door was to be securely fastened, then the middle door between the rooms was to be opened; the white men were to rush from the room in which they were concealed into that occupied by the Indians, and then their capture would be a very easy matter—as they thought. It was a very neat little plan, and looked well, but there was one objection to it—it didn't pan out worth a cent. The Indians, eleven in number, approached the house; they were invited to walk in, which invitation was accepted, as it was evidently their intention to walk in whether they were invited or not; the outside door to the room was closed and fastened; the signal was given; the door between the two rooms was opened; the white men rushed with a yell into the room which was occupied by the Indians, and—captured the whole posse? Not much. The greasy-skinned, slippery devils shed their blankets, dived down among the legs of the white men, slipped out like so many eels, burst open the door and were out of the room like a flash, and all the white men had to show for their stratagem was the lodgement of a slug in the wrist or one of their own number—Mr. James H. Peters—which was brought about by the accidental discharge of a gun during the melee in the room. The Indians were followed out of the house by the whites who blazed away at them as they ran toward the river. Two or three of the Indians were killed and one wounded; one was captured, having been brought down " on the wing " by a shot which should have been better aimed.

The whites then hastily got their wagons together, put the wounded Indian in one of them, and started back to Fontenelle, being very anxious to vacate that particular section of the country before the Indians who had made their escape from the house should reach the Pawnee camps, and tell the tribe of the fracas. The whites "stood not upon the order of their going, but went at once, rattling over the level prairie road at a deucedly rapid pace. They had not proceeded far before the wounded Indian gave evidence of being dead. He was closely examined by those in the wagon, who agreed unanimously that he was defunct—that he would never again smash up a brass clock for the purpose of getting the wheels to hang in his ears, nor rip up a feather bed in order to get a substitute for a blanket. He was a goner, and as it would not pay to haul dead Indians, the wagon was driven to the bank of the Elkhorn, near which the road ran, the corpse was picked up and pitched into the river. As soon as the supposed-to-be-dead Indian struck the water, he dived down and swam under water for the opposite bank, and it was then discovered that he had been playing "possum," and that he was better than a dozen dead men yet. But even an Indian cannot stay under water all the time; he must come up to breath, and when that red rascal's head broke the surface of the stream, as he came up to get a whiff of air, a load of buckshot was deposited in the back portion of his cranium by a white man who never could appreciate a practical joke, and had but a poor opinion of jokers, whether white, black, or red. The buckshot was evidently too heavy a load for the Indian to carry conveniently, for he never reached the other side of the river alive.

It did not take many days for the news with regard to the killing of the Indians at West Point to be carried to every part of the Terriory, and the entire country was in a blaze of excitement. It was generally thought that the Pawnees would at once declare war against the whites, and the outlying settlements were supposed to be in danger of immediate extermination. Governor Black issued orders to the few militia companies then organized, to hold themselves in readiness to move at a moment's notice, and muskets were shipped to the different settlements, with orders for the immediate organization of other companies. The settlers along the Elkhorn river flocked to Fontenelle, which village was turned into a military camp. The growing crops were neglected, and suffered much damage thereby. Pickets were thrown out during the day, and a cordon of sentinels surrounded the place at night. All the ammunition was collected together, and pewter teapots, teaspoons, etc., were moulded into bullets. Blunderbusses which had done good service in patriot hands during the revolutionary war, and which had not been loaded nor cleaned since, were dragged forth and furbished up. Old sabres which had figured prominently on "muster days" celebrated by the forefathers of their present owners, were produced, and measures adopted for the purpose of inducing them to leave their scabbards, from which they had not been drawn for years. It was reported every day for a week that ten thousand Indians were approaching the town fully attired in the traidtional war paint and feathers, and in consequence of these cheerful stories the people were constantly kept in a pleasant state of exciting suspense. At night each bush or shrub would be transformed into a stealthily approaching redskin.

A week of this sort of life drifted by, and no attack had been made. By this time a force of about two hundred men had gathered in and about Fontenelle, and it was then resolved by the officials of the Territory that it would be a fine stroke of policy to cross the Elkhorn, follow the trail of of the Indians until they were overtaken, and then and there attack them and administer a lesson which they would not soon forget. A sufficient number of wagons were provided, with the necessary camp equipage and a large amount of provisions (several barrels of whisky being included in the latter), and on the 5th day of July the force moved across the river, and went into camp on Maple creek, a few miles from Fontenelle. Gov. Black accompanied the expedition, of which he was the commander-in-chief, though the battalion was under the direct command of Col.— since Major General—Thayer, which gentleman had served in the Mexican difficulty, and was consequently supposed, by a credulous public, to be thoroughly conversant with the art of war. At this time I cannot remember the names of all the officers of the various companies, but of that from Fontenelle Wm. Kline was Captain, James A. Bell, First Lieutenant, and Wm. Flack, Second. Capt. Hazen commanded the Fremont company, J. J. Turton the one from North Bend, and Peter Reed that organized in Richland precinct. Capt. Bob Howard commanded the Omaha gun squad, and Lieut. Robinson 50 U. S. dragoons. The late General Samuel R. Curtis also accompanied the expedition, but took no active part in its management, although he, no doubt, rendered much service in the way of practical suggestions. I shall never forget the appearance that military organization presented when on the march. We had a mounted force of about sixty men, and the remainder of the two hundred rode in wagons. When every thing was in readiness for breaking camp in the morning, Col. Thayer would take position and give the order: "At ten-t-i-o-n, bat-tal-i-o-n! For-w-a-r-d, m-a-r-c-h!" the last word of command being pronounced in an indiscribable squeal, about two tones higher than Watchel's "high C."

Our mounted force always rode at the head of the columns, preceded by a few scouts, a considerable distance in advance. The sun beat down upon us with terrible force, and the sandy stretches of country over which we passed, at intervals, threw out an immense amount of heat. Our horses were very poor and weak, and the excessive heat together with the heavy loads, soon began to tell on them, and consequently the progress made was very slow indeed. We had no roads, as the country had not yet been surveyed, and no settlements had been made. We struck the trail of the Indians and followed it steadily, over hills, through valleys, and across streams, which last named were always mirey. Here we would generally be delayed somewhat, as a bridge of some description was required before we could get the wagons across. A force would be set to work to cut brush, while another would mow down the heavy slough grass. The brush would be thrown into the stream, the grass piled on the brush, and then if the banks were very steep, the horses would be unhitched from the wagons, which would be let down by ropes, and then drawn up the opposite bank by the teams which had been previously taken across. Notwithstanding the many difficulties to be encountered, we usually traveled as far in one day as the Indians we were pursuing would march in three, it being an easy matter to locate the places where they had camped each night, these encampments being about seven miles apart. The utmost precaution against surprise was observed when, at the close of a long tedious day, a convenient spot for a camp would be selected, the wagons coralled, and the animals turned out to graze. At an early hour in the night, sentinels would be posted all around the camp, and relieved every two hours. After about a week's travel, during which we had not seen a human being, excepting those of our own party, we came one evening upon a single Indian lodge. We knew that we could not be very far behind the Indians, as the last few camps we had passed gave an unmistakable signs of having been but recently vacated, and when this lodge was discovered, it was surrounded at once, and found to be occupied by "Jim Dick," an under chief among the Omahas, who told us that the Pawnees had been joined by the Omaha and Ponca tribes, and that with this increase of their numbers, there were at least 5,000 Indians in the party we were in pursuit of, and that they would encamp that night about seven or eight miles farther on, having occupied the camp at which we found Jim Dick's lodge, the night previous, he having laid over one day's tramp on account of his squaw being sick. This somewhat startling news called forth a hurried consultation. Five thousand Indians could utterly annihilate our force of two hundred undisciplined and poorly armed men, provided the Indians were disposed to fight. Jim Dick told us that the Omahas would not join the Pawnees as they wished to remain at peace with the whites, but it was impossible to say what the Poncas would do. It was finally determined to go forward. The Omaha and his squaw were compelled to go with us under guard, in order to prevent the news of our approach being conveyed to the Indians, in camp.

It was nearly night when we came upon the lodge, and we proceeded but a mile or so before going into camp. Arrangements were made to start out as silently as possible, at three o'clock the next morning. After supper had been disposed of, the cooking utensils and camp equppage were re-loaded, and every thing made ready for a start as soon as the signal should be given. The arms were put in as good condition as possible; bullets were moulded, and each man was instructed with regard to his duties. It was a misty moon-light night. The camp was near the banks of the Elkhorn, whose waters, rising in the far off Black Hills, at the foot of the Rocky Mountains, rippled past with a monotonous sound. Occasionally the sharp cry of the coyote would be heard, as he wandered forth on a marauding expedition, or the hoot of the owl would break suddenly on the night air. The sentinels paced up and down through the tall grass, watching with vigilant eye and prepared to give notice at the earliest approach of danger. The tired animals nipped the rich grass, which abounded in the greatest profusion, keeping close to the wagons, as they always do when away from the settlements, evidently being taught by instinct that their safety depends upon keeping close to their masters. Orders were given for the fires to be extinguished at an early hour, and the men gathered about the wagons in little groups, and talked in low tones of what the coming day would bring forth. There was but little sleeping among us that night, but few jokes, and no boisterous laughter. It will be seen at a glance that the situation was not particularly exhilarating nor inspiring. We were a hundred miles or so out on the plains, shut off from all chance of reinforcement. We were in pursuit of, and expected to attack the Pawnee tribe, numbering 3,500 in all, and this tribe we found on coming up with it, to be reinforced by nearly as many more, so that if they were all "on the fight," there would be at least 2,000 braves for us to attack, and we were then within a few miles of that body of Indians who were quietly encamped and resting in blissful ignorance of our proximity.

At 3 o'clock in the morning the camp was aroused, and in a very short time we were on the move. Orders were issued in a low tone as we passed rapidly along. The trail ran near the river bottom, on the table-land adjoining, and we met with no obstacles whatever until daylight, when we came to a small stream which ran out from the bluffs and into the river. The scouts approached this stream carefully, for it was thought the Indian camp could not be far away. The creek was skirted with timber, which shielded our approach; and when the stream was reached, the Indian camp was seen on the opposite side, near where it ran into the river. A large extent of ground was covered by the lodges, and here and there Indians were to be seen gliding about, entirely unconscious of our approach. In a very few moments, however, we were discovered, and the camp vanished like magic, and in an incredibly short space of time the wide river bottom stretching out before us was swarming with redskins, some mounted, some on foot, but all striving, shouting and yelling, to make their escape. They leveled their lodges to the ground, but did not attempt to take them away; they thought only to save themselves. The Omahas did not run, neither did they strike their tents, but remained in them knowing that they had no reason to fear the whites. Our mounted force crossed the stream at once and followed up the flying Indians, but some time was lost in getting the wagons across the mirey stream. Finally the entire force, wagons and all, were safely landed on the western side of the creek, and moved up the river at once. The tall slough grass through which we passed concealed a good many of the weaker ones among the Indians, who, finding themselves unable to keep up with the others, had dropped down in the rank grass, hoping to be passed by. On either side of us could be heard the cries and yells of papooses, who had been thrown away by the frightened squaws, in their endeavors to "travel light." Small dogs, pet badgers, wolves, and "sich," had also been left by their masters to shirk for themselves, and they added their voices to the noise and confusion. It was a lively time. The sun had just risen, and was tipping the tops of the hills and the trees along the river with golden splendor. In a very short time not an Indian was to be seen, where but half an hour before hundreds and thousands had swarmed. They had taken shelter among the willows on the river bank, and in the breaks along the bluffs on either side of it.

But they did not escape us. An under chief of the Pawnees, a fat old codger, who was trying to get away on foot, was overtaken by a horseman who shot at him and missed him, but just as he had secured a better aim for a second attempt, the Indian threw up his hands and surrendered. He was told to call his tribe together for a parley immediately, or he would be murdered in cold blood. The Indian was very glad of this chance for saving his life, and he at once set up a series of terrific yells, in answer to which one redskin would show himself at this place, another at that, and then after an interchange of yells and calls, the Indians gradually approached our prisoner, who explained to them that a parley with the "Chemokee man" was of the utmost importance at that particular juncture.

By this time our scattered forces had collected together; the wagons were correlled; a line of battle formed, with the six-pound brass piece in front of it, and the horsemen on the flanks. When the Indians, who were lurking about, discovered the full strength, or weakness rather, of the force they had been running from, they left their hiding places and approached us quite readily. They were ordered to keep a respectful distance in front, and only the chiefs were allowed to come to the wagons. The Indian force constantly received additions to its numbers, and before an hour had passed, we were confronted by about 2,000 redskins. The Pawnee chiefs were told that they could have their choice—give up the braves who had been engaged in the robbing and burning about West Point (for it was found that but a small party had been engaged in those depredations); pay the expenses of the expedition out of certain moneys due them from the government, or—fight us. One of the chiefs, a black, scowling fellow, with a sort of sheep thief look about him, wanted to fight us. He said that he had two hundred and fifty braves, and he knew he could clean us out, but the older and wiser heads of the tribe had been to Washington—that moral city of which we are all so proud;—they had held big pow-wows with the Great Father; they had gained a somewhat correct idea of the numbers of the whites, and of the power and majesty of the nation which we, with our single brass gun represented; and last but not least, those old coveys had a very distinct recollection of that exploit of Gen. Harney at Ash Hollow, and they begged of that bloodthirsty, belligerent young devil to "abate the ardor of his wrath," "for," said they—said those old sages, "if you do kill off this pusillanimous looking crowd of palefaces, you have not gained anything, for the Great Father at Washington will soon hear of it and he will send out more soldiers than there are sands on the Elkhorn, and we will be wiped from the face of the earth.''

It was finally arranged, after several hours had been occupied in the discussion of the matter, that the terms proposed by us would be acceded to, and then began a hunt for the Indians who had been raising Cain back in the settlements. By the middle of the afternoon we had seven young fellows tied behind one of our wagons, and we were moving off toward a suitable place to encamp for the night. Each of the head chiefs had attached his "sign manuel" to a portentious looking document which set forth in the most grandiloquent terms the fact that the individuals whose crosses were thereunto attached, regretted exceedingly the depredations which had been committed by certain unruly and headstrong young men of the Pawnee tribe of Indians, and that they, the undersigned, authorized the keeping back from certain moneys due the tribe from the government, a sufficient amount to defray the expenses of the expedition, and the signers further agreed that they would make no effort to release the seven young men who had been turned over to our tender mercies, no matter what we chose to do with them.

When the young Indians were given up to us, a squaw belonging to one of them, insisted on being allowed to go with her brave, and when this request was denied, she screamed and cried, tore the hair out of her head by great handfulls, threw her arms around the young fellow's neck, and gave way to the most violent grief. She was dragged away from him with difficulty, and we then proceeded on our way, traveling but a few miles before going into camp. One of the prisoners seemed to be suffering a great deal from some cause, and upon one of our doctors making an examination, it was found he had been shot through the body, and that the wound was mortifying. He was one of the party of eleven who had been shut up in the room at West Point, and as he ran off, after getting away from the house, he had been shot by one of the whites, but was not so seriously injured but that he was able to reach the Pawnee camp, but since that time his wound had been getting more and more painful, each day. The doctor said he would not live to reach the settlements, and he was therefore set free and told to go back to his tribe. He was found the next morning a short distance from camp, dead.

We enjoyed a happy, easy time the afternoon and night after the conference with the Indians, naturally supposing that all danger was now past, and that we could return home at once. It was arranged that we should proceed up the Elkhorn a few miles further, then travel in a southerly direction until we struck the head of Beaver Creek, and then follow down that stream to its intersection with the Loup Fork, follow the Loup until we came to the Platte, and then keep along the Platte until we reached the settlements. We had a beautiful camp that night. Huge cottonwood, walnut and elm trees spread their branches over our heads. A noisy little stream rippled at our feet, and the ground was covered with a rich green carpet of nature's weaving. Our minds were free from care or the apprehension of danger for the first time for many days, and we thoroughly enjoyed our pleasant surroundings. In due time, a supper of black coffee, fat bacon, molasses, and a certain kind of hot bread, peculiar to the plains, was prepared and eaten with a relish. The bread referred to was made of dough, composed of flour, water, salt and soda, mixed up tough and then dropped into a frying pan half full of hot grease. It requires the stomach of an ostrich, or a very healthy man, to digest it, and it would kill the oldest man in America in three weeks time if he should eat it and follow sedentary pursuits. As it requires a considerable amount of fat to cook bread in this way, it is looked upon as rather a rare treat, something as "duff" is aboard ship. The usual way of preparing bread on the plains is to mix up batter and make "slap-jacks." It is expected that after a man has beeen on the plains for a week, he will be able to "flop" a slap-jack over in a frying pan, when one side is done, without the aid of a knife, and when he has been out a month, he is supposed to be able to take hold of the frying pan handle, throw the half-done slap-jack over a covered wagon, run around to the other side with his frying pan, and catch the descending mass, dough side down. The old hands allow a beginner just a month in which to acquire this accomplishment, and if he is unable to go through with it without doubling the slap-jack up in the pan when he catches it, at the end of that time, he is considered a discouraging failure.

As I said before, we were happy. As the sun sank to rest, and the twinkling stars came out one by one, and the moon rose bright and clear, our camp presented a beautiful picture. A chain of sentinels surrounded it, but they were not so anxious or watchful as they necessarily were when upon guard previous to our coming up with the Indians. The song and jest passed around, and the hours slipped pleasantly by until it was time to "turn in." Then blankets were spread under the wagons, and as the moon looked down upon us, lighting up the scene with a mellow haze, we dropped off to sleep with the music of the rippling of waters and the chirp of a thousands of crickets, hidden in the grass, sounding in our ears.

We were roused up at early hour the next morning, and in a short time our cavalcade was on the move. After marching a few miles we reached a high point of ground, from which a magnificent and picturesque scene burst upon the view. Far off to the northwest we could trace the windings of the Elkhorn by the timber upon its banks, while here and there could be seen small streams which found their way from the highlands across the broad river bottoms. At our feet was seen the Indian camp, now a scene of active commotion, for they had just discovered our approach, and were rapidly gathering their herds of ponies from the neighboring hills. It was a mutual surprise. We supposed the Indians would remain the night previous at the place where the pow wow was held, and they probably thought we had turned back that morning, intending to go home by the route we had come.

We were in for it now. We wanted to go in a direction which would bring us very near the Indian camp, and if they were disposed to fight us, we would gain nothing by turning aside now. It was decided that we should get everything ready to repel an attack, move along as though the Indians were not there, and trust to fate for the rest Our six prisoners were tied together and then fastened by a rope to one of the wagons, behind which they walked quietly along, surrounded by a mounted guard. We did not go through the camp, but passed along one side of it. A few squaws and pappooses came out to see us as we moved along, but the Indians generally remained about their tents. Among the squaws who had come out from the camp, was the one before spoken of as having torn her hair and exhibited such great grief at being separated from her brave the day before, and when the wagon behind which the prisoners were tied, come up, this squaw rushed among them and gave her Indian a knife, with which he stabbed himself in the breast, and fell heavily to the ground. Of course the wagon stopped at once, and the attention of the guards was taken up with the wounded Indian, whom they supposed to be bleeding internally, as but little blood was to be seen about the wounds, although a reddish looking matter, similar to blood in appearance, oozed from each corner of his mouth. As the guards were doing what they could to assist the Indian who had stabbed himself, his treacherous squaw secured the knife and cut the ropes which bound the prisoners together, and away they sprang like a flash, all the guards but one running after them, firing upon them as they ran. Meanwhile, the wounded Indian had stretched out, his eyes sunk into his head, and he gave every indication of being dead, while that squaw of his hung over him, indulging in wild expressions of grief. When she saw that the guards were some distance from the wagon, she gave her buck the signal, and he jumped to his feet as agile as a cat, and started to run. But he did not go far. One guard had remained to keep an eye on the corpse, and when that corpse attempted to run away, contrary to the customs and habits of corpses generally, the guard drew up his rifle and called, "halt!" The Indian halted, and it was then found that the wound which he had inflicted upon himself was only skin-deep, and that he had red ochre in his mouth, by means of which he had created the impression that blood was oozing from between his lips. He was immediately recaptured, tied behind the wagon, and the procession moved on.

We proceeded about a mile, took up position on a high hill, and then stopped for a consultation. The guards who pursued the escaped prisoners had returned to the command, and reported that they had either killed or wounded all the prisoners except the one which had been recaptured. This was well enough, but in the excitement of the chase they had popped over an Omaha, (down among whose tents the prisoners ran), and had also killed an Omaha pony. The indications just at that time were that we had cut out more work for ourselves than we could get through with conveniently. It was reasonable to suppose that the Pawnees had been thoroughly roused by the occurrences of the last half hour, and if the Puncas and Omahas would join them, it was quite probable that they would "go back" on the agreement of the previous day. The Omahas had acted very fairly thus far, utterly refusing to have anything to do with trouble into which the Pawnees had brought themselves, as they considered it "none of their funeral," but it was a difficult matter to decide what they would do now, since one of their braves had been wounded and a pony killed. We were on a high hill, about a mile from the Indian camp, with no chance to get wood or water, and it would be a very easy matter for us to be surrounded and starved to death. The prospects was somewhat gloomy and discouraging.

While we were deliberating over the matter, we saw a procession of Indians leave the Omaha camp and approach us, " with stately step and slow," which procession proved to be composed of fifty of the wise heads among the Omahas. They marched in single file without a sound being heard, and as they slowly approached us, we could see that their minds were filled with serious thoughts. They were decorated in a peculiar manner, their costumes indicating that they were prepared for either war or peace, as circumstances might seem to dictate.

But they didn't fight us, our cheek and our extraordinary conversational powers saved us for the second time. We reasoned with those chiefs; we talked as we had never talked before. We portrayed in brilliant and glowing colors the evils which would result to the red-skins generally in case the Omahas and the Poncas joined with the Pawnees in declaring war against us. We dwelt especially upon the immense resources possessed by the whites; of their great facilites for the carrying on of a prolonged and bloody warfare. We deprecated the accidental shooting of the Omaha, promising to hang the man who had fired the unfortunate shot. We made mention of the fact that the Omahas had been at peace with us ever since the first settlement of the Territory. We had regular details made to talk to those old chaps who had one side of their villainous looking countenances painted red and the other black, and as soon as one detail of men would be exhausted, another took their place, and we outwinded them. Their desire for war gradually cooled, (nothing could withstand the avalanche of talk which we hurled at their devoted heads,) and they finally agreed that if we would leave medicines for the wounded Indians, and pay for the pony we had killed, they would let us off. To this condition we assented cheerfully, and as the Poncas had signified their intention to do as the Omahas decided to do in the matter, the Pawnees concluded that they would not fight us alone. We left a horse for the Indian whose pony had been killed, and we were allowed to move on. We did not camp very early that night. Every mile that we traveled, put that much distance between us and the Indians, and we were seized with a desire to make that as great as possible before stopping for the night. We were not all afraid to encamp in their immediate vicinity, but it occurred to us that perhaps in view of all the facts it would be better if we were some distance from the Indian camp that night. We thought they would like it better.

Soon after leaving the scene of our conference, we struck Beaver Creek, and followed along its course. We traveled late that night, and did not go into camp until near midnight. Keeping along Beaver Creek, we came in due time to its intersection with the Loup Fork, at the Mormon settlement of Genoa, before spoken of. Here we were cordially received by the Mormons, who looked upon us as a band of brave and noble men who had sacrificed home and home comforts for the nonce, going forth with our lives in our hands to do battle in defense of the unprotected settlements, and shield them from the devastating torch of the savage.

Leaving the Mormon camp—in a manner becoming a band of heroes—we journeyed down the Loup Fork, and reached the German town of Columbus that night, at which place we went into camp. We also indulged in a high old time—we felt that the Indians were now safe from any murderous designs which we may have harbored against them, and we rejoiced to know it. We left one company of our command at Columbus, it having been organized there, and after leaving that village, our force decreased very rapidly. We were formally disbanded at Columbus, the different companies being allowed to return to the various settlements from whence they came by the nearest and most practicable routes. We were told that each company commander would receive the pay due his company, and that the members of the company would be paid by him. It was supposed that the government would enforce the contract we had made with the Indians, keep back enough funds to pay the expenses of the expedition, and that we would receive the money which was due us. But the Government recoiled on us, paid the the Indians all that was due them, and we were left to whistle for our pay. We are whistling yet.

Thus ended the Pawnee war.

MURDERS AND MURDER TRIALS.

A BRIEF SKETCH OF THE IMPORTANT MURDER TRIALS IN THE COUNTY.

There have been fewer men killed within the boundaries of Washington county since its settlement than one would naturally expect under the circumstances. In 1858 a man named Blackwood, living near De Soto, was arrested on account of a difficulty he had had with a man named Lamb, in which he cut the latter with an axe. He was committed to jail to await trial before the District Court of the Territory, but broke jail, went to his house, and there barricaded himself. He shot at Harvey Estes, who happened to be passing by, whereupon a warrant was issued for his arrest and placed in the hands of Wm. Frazier, Deputy Sheriff, who, in endeavoring to serve it, shot Blackwood. Frazier was tried and acquitted on the ground that the killing was justifiable homicide.

In 1859 Henry Seevers, while under the influence of liquor, stabbed an Englishman by the name of Bovee, in a saloon at De Soto, with a butcher knife, killing him. Seevers was arrested and bound over to the next term of court, but the grand jury failed to find an indictment against him and he was released.

In 1861 Hiram Frazier, a boy thirteen years old, shot a German who had said the boy stole a whip, the German dying within a few hours from the effects of the wound. The boy was sentenced to be hung, but the Governor commuted the sentence to imprisonment for life. Young Frazier served three years in the jail at Omaha, when he was pardoned out. The family went west after his release and settled on the Republican, where it is reported they were all massacred by Indians.

In the winter of 1869-70, one McAuley, a clerk at the Quimby House, was killed by John Jones, head cook at the hotel. McAuley was running away from Jones, when the latter threw a butcher's cleaver at him, the weapon passing between McAuley's arm and body, severing the main artery of the arm. The wounded man ran some distance into a saloon where he bled to death before the startled occupants of the establishment knew what was the matter with him. Jones was tried in June, 1870, before Judge Crounse, now Representative in congress, when the jury disagreed, standing eleven to one. After they had been discharged it was found that the one juryman, who had stood out alone, was insane, and he was at once removed to the asylum at Lincoln. At the second trial, Jones was sentenced to ten years imprisonment. He was ably defended by Col. James W. Savage, now Judge of the Third district, and John Carrigan, Esq., of Blair, E. F. Gray, Esq., of Fremont, being the prosecuting attorney for the district at that time.

February 8th, 1875, Phillip Kleinburg, in company with a neighbor, Herman Brandert, left his home on the Brainard farm, a mile north of Fontenelle, to haul wheat to Nickerson station, three miles distant on the Elkhorn Valley railroad. Returning three hours later, about noon, he found his wife, whom he had left in the morning well and hearty, lying in the snow a few feet north of the house, with three terrible gashes in her throat. The ground where her head had evidently been lying when the wounds were inflicted, was covered with blood, and the body was then partially cold, indicating that death had ensued at least half an hour before. He ran over to his nearest neighbor, Mr. Christy Achilles, informed him of the horrible discovery, and Mr. Achilles at once went to Fontenelle and summoned help. Tracks in the freshly fallen snow were traced from the body to the house of Chris Hamming, half a mile to the east, and corresponding tracks—apparently made with buffalo overshoes—were discovered leading from Hamming's house, to that of Kleinburg, and a pair of buffalo overshoes on the soles of which were snow and ice, were found in Hamming's house. Willard Randall, a young man nineteen years of age, had occupied this house alone for several days, and he was arrested on suspicion of being the murderer. He was tried at Blair, before Judge Samuel Maxwell, in November, 1875, District Attorney Connell, prosecuting, and Col. Savage, of Omaha, and John Carrigan, Esq., of Blair, defending. The jury disagreed and a change of venue to Douglas county was obtained. In March, 1876, the case was tried before Judge Griffey, of the Sixth district—Judge Savage being incapacitated by reason of his former connection with the case—and a verdict of murder in the second degree returned by the jury. The prisoner was sentenced to ten years imprisonment and is now serving out his term. In the second trial Mr. Connell was assisted by John C. Cowin, of Omaha, and Mr. Carrigan secured the services of Charles H. Brown, of Omaha, as assistant counsel for the defense.

Last May Henry King, a German, was killed by Minor Milton, under the following circumstances: There had been some feeling of unfriendliness existing between Milton and two Swedes, named respectively John Christian and Jans Jenson, on the one side, and Henry and Edward King on the other. The parties all lived in the same neighborhood, some two miles south of Blair, and were in Blair the day of the killing, attending court. The King brothers left town in the evening in their wagon to go home, and a short time afterwards Milton, Christian, and Jensen left in the wagon of the latter. It was not proven that they knew the Kings were ahead of them, but it was shown that after getting a few miles out they came within sight of the Kings and at once whipped up their horses in pursuit. The Kings gave rein to their horses, and finally drove into a farm house, about seven miles southwest of Blair, for protection. Milton's team was close behind them. The Kings jumped out of their wagon and started to run. Henry King was pursued by Milton, who struck him over the head with a heavy club, breaking his skull, and knocking him senseless to the ground. Edward King was also knocked down by either Milton or Christian, while Jensen held the team. Henry King died from the effect of his injuries, but his brother recovered. The assaulting party were arrested, Milton found guilty of murder in the first degree, at a special term of court, held by Judge Savage in the latter part of May, and was sentenced to be hung September 22d, 1876. Christian was tried and acquitted, and a *nolle* was entered by the State in the case of Jensen. John Carrigan, assisted by his law partner, L. W. Osborn, conducted the defense, and appealed the case of Milton to the Supreme Court, which does not meet until the second Monday in September. District Attorney W. J. Connell conducted the prosecution.

RAILROADS.

The Sioux City & Pacific, Omaha & Northwestern, and Elkhorn Valley Railroads.

In 1864 was organized the Northern Nebraska Air Line Railroad Company, but nothing was done in the way of constructing a road. In 1867, the company was re-organized, consisting of John S. Bowen, John A. Unthank, Dean C. Slader, Jessie T. Davis and T. P. Kennard, the object being to build a railroad from DeSoto to Fremont. A land grant of seventy-five sections of land was donated the company by the State, in aid of the enterprise, and a temporary line was built from De Soto to the present site of Blair. In 1868, the company disposed of its franchise to John I. Blair and associates, who, the following year, completed the Sioux City & Pacific road from the Missouri immediately east of Blair to Fremont, there forming a junction with the Union Pacific and Elkhorn Valley roads. A year or two afterwards the De Soto branch, or "plug" as it was called in derision, was taken up, having never been operated. Considerable bad feeling was gotten up among the residents of the county in consequence of this abandonment of the original design to make De Soto the eastern terminus of the road, in Washington County, but that soon passed off. County aid to the amount of $75,000 was voted the Sioux City & Pacific road, in 1869. This road has been successfully operated ever since its completion. Mr. Scott Bryan is agent for the company at Blair.

Evidently satisfied with the result of aiding in the construction of railroads, the people of the county, in 1870, voted in favor of issuing bonds to the amount of $125,000 in favor of the Omaha & Northwestern, and in 1872, this line was completed as far as Herman, along the eastern line of the county. This summer it is being built to Tekamah, the county seat of Burt County, and will eventually be pushed many miles farther to the Northwest. Mr. Charles Willard is the company's agent at Blair.

The Elkhorn Valley road does not run through Washington county, but is built in the valley of the Elkhorn river, on the west side of that stream, from Fremont to Wisner, affording railroad transportation to the western portion of the county, the river being bridged.

ROCKPORT.

WHAT IT WAS IN ITS PALMY DAYS—A TOWN OF THE PAST.

Time was when Rockport, situated on the Missouri River, about a dozen miles above Omaha, was one of the best known and most flourishing little towns in Nebraska. It was first settled in 1657, Wm. H. Russell, still a prominent citizen of the county, and President of the Old Settlers Association, now residing near DeSoto, being one of its founders. J. P. Burkett, Hawley Bros., David and Stephen Neal, and Dr. Lewis were also among the early settlers of Rockport. David Neal still lives there. Mr. Burkett lives at Yankton, and was at one time agent for the Yankton Sioux.

Rockport boasted at one time, a fine, large hotel building, but for some reason it was never furnished, and was finally moved down to Florence. It was built by the Town Company. A splendid body of hardwood timber surrounded the town, and extensive stone quarries were opened and successfully worked, in the vicinity. But the timber was cut down by the Union Pacific railroad company, who also bought the quarries, I believe, and as there was no agricultural country surrounding the town near enough to be tributary to it, the settlement to a considerable extent, rapidly dwindled away after the stone and timber interest passed out of the hands of private parties, until now its glory is a thing entirely of the olden time, having passed into the keeping of tradition. Its lumber and shingle mills, which did a flourishing business, have been removed, and silence and solitude now reign where once were beautiful homes and the busy hum of industry. In the long ago, the heavy timber and deep ravines surrounding the settlement, afforded excellent facilities for the hanging of horse thieves, which facilities were frequently utilized, until finally an extensive and enterprising band of lawless horse-fanciers who made their headquarters near De Soto, were effectually broken up. It is a significant fact that the county lost a number of its most prominent and enterprising citizens in consequence of the disorganization of this band of horse thieves.

FORT CALHOUN.

Thd Founders of the Town — "Jumping" the Town Site — The First Court — Doings of the Claim Club — List of the "Old Tmers."

The town site of Fort Calhoun was claimed early in the summer of 1854, by John Goss, Senior; who lived and owned a farm just opposite on the Iowa side of the Missouri river, and was soon after donated by him, (except two shares, one for himself and one for his son John Goss, Jr.,) to a company consisting of Casady & Test, Addison Cochran and H. C. Purple, of Council Bluffs, and Mark W. Izard, Governor of the Territory. Andrew J. Poppleton and Hadley D. Johnson, prospective residents of Omaha.

This company built a cabin upon the site of the old Fort, near the magazine, (which was a solid stone structure; 10x12 feet in size, and with walls two feet thick,) had the boundaries of the town surveyed and a plat drawn, and divided among themselves. About this time, Maj. Ansel Arnold, (father of Brice Arnold, the present sheriff of Washington county,) took a claim one quarter of a mile south, and moved his family from where the present town of Florence now is—which was then in Washington county—on to it, bringing with him, a Mr. George W. Nevell and family, who were engaged by the Town Company to occupy their cabin and hold the claim. In January of that year, the boundaries of the county were by act of the Legislature, then in session, changed, and the County Seat located at Fort Calhoun, and the county fully organized by the appointment of Stephen Cass, Probate Judge; George W. Nevell, Recorder, and Thos. J. Allen, Sheriff. The county was included in the First Judicial District of the Territory, over which Chief Justice Fenner Furgeson was appointed to preside.

In March 1855, Mr. E. H. Clark, now a resident of Blair, was employed by the Town Company to survey off the town into lots and blocks, and plat the same, which he did, and had one hundred lithographs printed, which were divided up by the company, and sent to their friends to advertise the town, as was customary in those days.

In June 1855, the first court was opened in the county in the claim cabin of the Town Company. It was presided over by the Hon. Fenner Furgeson, with Maj. J. W. Paddock, now of Omaha, as clerk, Gen. E. Estabrook, U. S. Prosecuting Attorney, and Thos. J. Allen, sheriff. The attorneys present were E. Estabrook, Andrew J. Poppleton, E. H. Clark, and J. McNeal Latham. The first case tried was that of Elias Wilcox vs. James M. Taggart, for claim jumping. The case was prosecuted by E. H. Clark, and defended by J. McNeal Latham, and was decided in favor of the plaintiff. It was for the land afterwards pre-empted and now owned by Wicox, being a valuable piece of timber five miles west of Fort Calhoun.

During this spring, several came into the neighborhood. At this time the settlement consisted of Anselam Arnold and family, Geo. W. Nevell and family, Wm. Connor and family, Stephen Cass and family, Orrin Rhodes and family, Thomas J. Allen and family, James Craig and family, Je se Estlock and family, Wm. Moore and family, James M. Taggart, E. H. Clark and several single men who have since left the country and not now remembered. There was on wed at this time in the entire precinct, only seven yoke of cattle and one span of horses, and in breaking prairie the settlers had to double teams, and consequently got but little breaking done that season.

In June of the year 1855 for the consideration of one-ninth interest in the town, E. H. Clark contracted with the proprietors to put up a building on the town site for a hotel; said building to be 24x48 feet, two stories high, and with an ell of the same dimensions; the structure to be of hewn logs and put up in good style. The contract was in writing, and as soon as the building was completed, each member of the company was to deed Mr. Clark by quit-claim his proportion of the lots to be taken indiscriminately from all parts of the town. He immediately, with six men, commenced the work of getting out the timber, boarding in the meantime with Major Arnold's family, and laboring under many disadvantages, both for want of skilled laborers and teams. The men were newly arrived from Virginia, none of whom had ever done manual labor, but were out of money and must do something; so had imposed themselves upon Mr. Clark as men from a timbered country, and used to such work, and as hands were not readily obtained in those days, he had to submit, paying them two dollars each per day and boarding them. For teams he hired a yoke of oxen from the settlers as they could spare them from their own work. What lumber was necessary for the building had to be obtained from Omaha (where a mill had been started) at $60 per thousand, and hauled a circuitous route by the old Mormon trail a distance of eighteen miles. As an additional incident to his trials, one morning at breakfast Mr. Clark was told by Mrs. Arnold that the last mouthful in the house was on the table. Maj. Arnold, who was absent for supplies, had been expected home the night before, but as he had not come, it was supposed that he could not get any team to come with. This proved to be the fact, and Mr. Clark procured two yoke of oxen and started at once for

Omaha for provisions, thinking he could bring back a load of lumber as soon as to make the trip without, which proved to be a sad mistake, for never having driven oxen before, he met with many mishaps, and by the hardest work, traveling all night through rain and mud, only reached sight of home at sunrise next morning, when the oxen ran away, upsetting the lumber and scattering the groceries all over the prairies, so that little was recovered but some bacon and a barrel of flour. He found the family standing outside the house anxiously looking for his return, having had nothing to eat since the morning before, and who expecting him early in the evening, had hopefully watched the entire night through, his men having taken care of themselves by going off to the neighbors and leaving Mrs. Arnold and her then small children entirely helpless.

About the 10th of August the claim cabin of the town company having been vacated, one Charles T. Davis, in a very unostentations manner moved in, and filed a claim on the town site and served a written notice upon Mr. Clark to quit tresspassing upon the claim. The latter notified the company of his action, and kept on drawing material on the ground for his building, and after three days Davis sued him for tresspass, fixing his damages at $100, for which he afterwards obtained judgment, and Clark paid it. Mr. Clark then notified the company that he should sell his material and leave unless they took steps to put the title out of controversy. They returned word for him to go on with the work and they would guarantee the title. A day or so after, while engaged with all the neighbors in raising the building, a number of the company, with some friends, ten or twelve in all, came up and wanted Clark to join them in removing Davis forcibly from the claim, which he declined to do. While parlying over the matter a man was seen going at full speed on horseback from the claim cabin towards DeSoto, and, as it was already known that the settlement at DeSoto was to back Davis in his attempt to hold the Calhoun town site (DeSoto being a rival), Clark told the company that the sooner they got over there the better, if they were going, for Davis would soon have help from DeSoto. They thought not, and still insisted that all the settlers around Calhoun were interested, and should go and assist. The talk was continued until dinner time, and then the party went off to dinner, and when returning, saw three wagon loads of armed men coming from DeSoto and going into the house with Davis. It was then thought by the representatives of the company useless to attack them, but they proposed that the entire party should go so as to show as strong a force as possible in order to scare Davis off, and that if he would not go, they would come up again with a stronger force when he was not expecting it, and put him off the claim. To this the settlers agreed, and all marched over to the house, and were drawn up in line in front of the door, which was closed. Col. Addison Cochran as spokesman knocked at the door, which was answered by Davis from within, demanding what they wanted. Cochran told him that he knew that claim belonged to the town company, and that they wanted him to peaceably leave it, and that if he did not, they should put him off by force. Davis' attorney—Potter C. Sullivan—replied, claiming some legal ground for Davis' action, and it was agreed that he should come outside and talk the matter over with Cockron. While they were talking, the door was opened, and some one from the inside said he would like to "put a bullet through Thompson,"—one of the party outside—whereupon some words passed when Thompson and the man making the remark, each drew their revolvers and fired at the same time, but neither shot took effect. The line was drawn up about twenty-five feet from the door, and as soon as these shots were fired, a dozen guns were seen pointing from the cabin, and shot after shot was fired upon Cochran and his retreating party, three of which shots took effect, one through the heart of John Goss, sr., killing him instantly; one through the arm of H. C. Purple, in the shoulders, so shattering it that it was two or three years before he recovered, and only after seven surgical operations had been performed by the most skilled surgeons of Chicago. Both of these parties were proprietors in the town site. The third shot took effect in the thigh of the Mr. Thompson who had the words with the man inside, but it was only a flesh wound, however, from which he soon recovered. When Mr. Goss fell, Mr. Clark was still standing before the door, and his escape was miraculous, as bullets whistled on every side. He immediately ran to Mr. Goss' assistance, and while holding his head, a number of shots were fired at him, and after laying him down and going in search of his son, who returned to the body with him, the occupants of the house kept firing at them, but with no effect, though not over fifty feet distant. The escape of the two men can only be accounted for by the excited condition of those who held the guns. The body of Goss was put in a wagon and conveyed to his home in Iowa, and there buried. This sad affair was a terrible blow to the little community, and none knew what would happen next, as it was feared such feelings were aroused that many more would be killed, by being waylaid or otherwise.

The night after this affray, Davis sent his attorney, Sullivan, to Omaha to compromise the matter, he doubtless fearing another attack. The town company agreed with Sullivan to arbitrate the right to the town site, and that all hostilities on both sides and all work on the site should be suspended until after the after the arbitration, which was to be by disinterested parties chosen, one from Bellvue, one from Nebraska City, and one from Glenwood. The time fixed was a month from that date, and when the time came the arbitrators could not be got together and, in fact, never did meet. Thus the matter rested until November, when Davis, who all the time had not felt safe, made a sale, or pretended sale, to Major Anselum Arnold, Thomas J. Allen, Jesse Esttock, and James M. Taggart, and they with Casady and Test, John Goss, Mrs. Goss, widow of John Goss, Sr., formed a new town company, taking Mr. Clark in as an equal proprietor providing he should go on and complete his hotel building according to the original contract, which he did, and in March, 1856, gave Col. George Stevens, then in the Douglas House at Omaha, a one-half interest in the building on condition he would move into it and open a hotel. This Col. Stevens did during that month, and the house was long celebrated as one of the best kept hotels in the west.

During this spring the town had assumed very considerable proportions. Buildings sprang up on every hand, among which was a grocery store, by W. H. Jacoby, which building still stands; a blacksmith shop, two saloons, and a number of dwellings. Among others those of N. Runyon, A. P. Allen, (both of whom still live in the town) and E. H. Clark. The latter's house was burned down on the morning of the 1st day of January, 1860, when the thermometer stood at 30° below zero—the coldest day ever witnessed since the State was settled. Through the spring and summer of 1856 dozens were coming to the town every day, the hotels and private houses were crowded continually and many had to go away for want of temporary accommodations. Alonzo Perkins and Perkins Allen came with a saw mill and put it up under the bluff, close to the old fort grounds, Lewis McBride and Frank Fithion built a large and commodious store and filled it with a fine stock of general merchandise. Mr. Clark built a law office, in which Geo. W. Nevell—who the fall before had been appointed postmaster—opened a postoffice with glass boxes, and all the paraphanalia of a first-class office. A four horse coach was put on the road between Omaha and Fort Calhoun by the Western Stage Company, and a rushing business was done in all branches of trade—particularly in town lots and land claims, the former ranging in price from one to five hundred dollars, according to location. A Court House was built by the subscription of the citizens, on one of the public squares, 16x20 in size, and in which the Hon. E. Wakely, now of Omaha, first presided as Judge, with Geo. W. Doane, also of Omaha, at present, as prosecuting attorney, Roger T. Beal clerk, and Orrin Rhodes sheriff, the bar present consisting of Kline & Clark and Clark Irvine, of this county, and A. J. Poppleton, E. Estabrook, and Jonas Seely, of Omaha. Claim jumping was common and many conflicts ensued therefrom—in some cases murder. In April one Isaiah Peterson jumped the claim of a Mr. Coon, having built a house in an out of the way place, where it was not known until he was occupying it. Mr. Coon went to see him and was there found dead soon afterwards with a bullet through his heart. Peterson claimed that he killed Coon in self defense, which was not believed. Nothing further is known however, about it. Peterson was arrested and indicted but made his escape before he had a trial as there was no place to confine him but in the Court House. Coon was buried on the spot where he was shot, and it was said by parties from the east when they went back home, that the country was so healthy that we had to kill a man to start a graveyard, Mr. Coon being the first man buried in the county. The claim is now the fine farm of Hans J. Rohwer, who purchased it of Geo. W. Homan, sr., now of Omaha, and he of the Coon heirs.

A claim club was organized at Fort Calhoun as well as in all other settlements, and on one occasion, soon after the killing of Coon, a stranger "squatted" on the claim of a member of the club, built a shanty, and was occupying the same when the club went in force and arrested him,

3

brought him into Calhoun and by the exhibition of a rope, extorted from him a promise to leave the country, which promise he fulfilled to the letter. In this peculiar line Fort Calhoun became somewhat noted, for soon after that another party was taken, on suspicion of being a hard character, to the Missouri river, crossed over to the Iowa side in a boat, and advised never to return, and has not since been seen in that vicinity. About the same time two horses were stolen from near Rockport by two men named Rowen and Brady who were captured and for safe keeping put in the jail at Omaha but before their trial were taken out by masked men, some of whom belonged at Calhoun, and hung to a tree, one of them the man named Brady, requesting that the rope be passed between his jaws instead of around his neck, which was done. Four of the parties implicated in this affair were arrested and imprisoned in Omaha, and after two ineffectual attempts to convict them were discharged. And very recently a prominent citizen received an anonymous letter giving him five days to leave the town or suffer the consequences. He went.

During the summer of 1856 preaching was had in the town once a month by the Rev. Mr. Collins, a Methodist minister located at Omaha. Services were held in the Court House, as was also the school and meetings of all kinds. A Sabbath school was started with eight or ten children of all ages and sizes and as many adults, with E. H. Clark as Superintendent the first year, after which Dr. J. P. Andrew was elected Supertendent and, with the exception of one year, (when a Mr. Davis served) he has held the position ever since, being re-elected each year by the unanimous vote of the school, and through his prompt attendance and efficiency, it is now one of the most flourishing Sabbath schools in the county. A day school was also started, with Miss Lucy Graham as teacher. Col. Geo. Stevens, P. N. Stilts, and E. H. Clark were elected a school committee, under the school law of the Territory.

During this season, the influx of immigration was so great and improvement so rapid that it would be impossible to give anything like a detailed account of all, but the most important enterprises to the town were the steam saw mill of Perkins & Allen, heretofore mentioned and the commencement of the steam grist mill, which was completed and put in operation in 1858 by Z. Vanier & Bro., and in 1861, passed into the hands of Elam Clark and Samuel Hale by virtue of a mortgage held by them. Samuel Hale, a year or so after sold his interest to Taylor Bradley, of La Porte, Indiana, and he a few years after sold to Elam Clark who thus became the sole proprietor, and he still owns and runs the mill. An incident, perhaps worth relating here, occurred in connection with this mill property. The Messrs. Vanier finding that they could not pay off the mortgage on the mill, conceived the idea that if they could get the machinery out of the county they could hold it, and that being the valuable part of the mill, they made the attempt by getting a large force to help them, and procuring teams from Omaha to assist, commencing one Saturday after 9 o'clock at night. They so far succeeded as to get the machinery all out and mostly on the road, some of it having got as far as

Florence, when they were stopped by writ of injunction and the machinery all recovered and put into the hands of a receiver (Mr. James Thompson) appointed by the court. Mr. Thompson replaced it in the mill and run the same until the termination of the suit which transferred the property from the Vaniers to Clark & Hale. Excitement over this matter ran high for a long time, some sympathizing and siding with the Vaniers' and others with Clark & Hale, and the community was pretty eqally divided between the two. The cause of this sympathy and division, however, dated back to the entry of the town site in 1857, at which time about half the citizens, with the Vaniers were on one side, and they still clung to them through the mill difficulty. This difference over the town arose from a conflict of town authorities. In January, 1856 the town was incorporated by act of the legislature as a city and a Mayor and Board of Aldermen authorized to be elected the following March and annually therefrom, and which were not elected until March, 1857. The land coming in market that year a board of trustees was quietly elected and organized under the general incorporation law of the Territory by Alonzo Perkins, the Voniers and their friends, who constituted the one side, and entered the town at the government land office in Omaha, claiming that as the Mayor and Board of Aldermen were not elected at the first election appointed in the act of incorporation, the charter was forfeited and they were not a legal body. The Mayor, however, filed *caveat* and contested the matter, and after a re-hearing was succesful, the entry of Board of Trustees being cancelled and the town was entered by Elam Clark, as Mayor, and the lots by him deeded to the several owners. This so embittered the two parties that it kept a division in the town for five years.

During this contest of the authorities over the town site, claim jumping was tried. Col. Stevens had built a residence on one of the most valuable lots in the west part of the town and, having temporarily moved out of it, a Mr. Elisha Aldrich, one of the opposite party, moved his family in and took possession, whereupon the Claim Club went to move him out. Mrs. Aldrich sat herself down in a chair and said they would have to "carry her out if they got her out," so the chair with Mrs. Aldrich in it was gently carried out of door and she was left sitting on the prairie. The house was locked up and was not invaded or molested neither was any claim jumping of any kind afterwards indulged in.

By this time so many settlers had come in that it would be impossible to enumerate all. Among those now remembered, however, in the precinct of Calhoun were Maj. Arnold and family, Geo. W. Nevell and family, Wm. Connor and family, Wm. Shipley and family, John Ryan and family, John Kelly and family, W. H. Russell and family, D. B. Hawley and family, James Goodrich and family, Orrin Rhodes and family, Thos. J. Allen and family Jesse Estlock and family, Hugh McNeely and family Mr. Johnson and family, James Craig, sr., and family, A. Reed and family, Wm. Moore and family, Dr. J. P. Andrew and family, Col. George Stevens and family, E. H. Clark and family, Daniel Franklin and family, N. Runyon and family, A. P. Allen and family, John Allen and family,

Robert Allen and family, Pat Stetts and family, Miss Mary Ann Tew and family, Ela Stetts and family, Perkins Allen and family, Alonzo Perkins and family, E. Aldrich and family, Wm. Frazier and family, Thos. Frazier and family, H. J. Rohwer and family, Geo. W. Doane and family, James Borland and family, W. B. Beals and family, Newton Clark and family, W. H. Jacoby, W. P. Rowford, James M. Piper, Chester Lusk, James S. Wiseman, Dean C. and Charles Slader, David McDonald, Chris Rathman, J. B. Kuony and family, Joel Neff, M. Gales, Levi Kline, Clark Irvine, James S. Riddler, Dan. W. Case, James L. Barbor, John and William Apple, A. S. Paddock, now United States Senator, Dwight A. Clark Michael Upton, Mr. Alexander (a noted Scotchman, who died at Calhoun in 1858), John Everheart, George Everheart and wife, Jacob Kreitter and family, C. Bannister and family, Geo. W. Homan, sr. and family, Paul Stallenburg and family Henry Frahm.

As stated previously the county seat of Washington county was located by act of legislature at Ft. Calhoun in 1855. Three years later by special legislative enactment, it was removed to De Soto; in 1861 it was again located at Calhoun, this time by a vote of the people, and in 1866 it was fixed at Blair—also by a public vote, and there it will probably remain permanently.

In May, 1856, the first Sunday School was organized and in 1857 there was a religious revival at Calhoun, De Soto and Fontenelle, at the same time, brought about, mainly by the earnest, zealous efforts of Rev. T. B. Lemon, then stationed at De Soto.

The following named lawyers have practiced their profession while residing at Fort Calhoun; E. H. Clark, Levi Kime, Clark Irvine, Geo. W. Doane, W. W. Toole, E. N. Gray. E. N. Grennell, and John D. Howe (now of Omaha.) Senator A. S. Paddock was admitted to the bar, while living at Calhoun, but did not practice. Judge L. Crounse, now our representative in Congress, located at Calhoun in 1857, upon being appointed to the third Judicial district. He still resides there and spends his time with his family, in their charming home, when not at Washington.

Dr. J. P. Andrews (still a resident of the town) Dr. Wm. Moore, and Dr. Charles Lawrence, are the only medical gentlemen who have taken up their abode at Calhoun.

Miss Cara Clark, now deputy county clerk, daughter of E. H. Clark, was the first child born in the town, that event occuring in May 1856.

DE SOTO.

LOCATED IN 1854—RELIGIOUS SERVICES UNDER DIFFICULTIES—BREAKING UP A BAND OF HORSE THIEVES—A TOWN SITE JUMPER.

The town of De Soto was incorporated by act of the legislature in March, 1855, having been laid out in the fall of the year previous by Dr. John Glover, Gen. J. B. Robinson, Potter C, Sullivan, (now a resident of Oregon, from which State he lacked only one vote of being sent to Congress) E. P. Stout, Wm. Clancy and others, Judge Jesse T. Davis locating there in the fall of 1855. In March, 1855, a charter was granted E. P. Stout to run a flat boat ferry across the Missouri. Again in January, 1856, a charter was granted to Wm. Clancy and P. C. Sullivan, to establish and run a steam ferry, and city bonds were voted to the amount of $30.000 to aid the enterprise, P. C. Sullivan being dispatched to the east for the purpose of disposing of the bonds and procuring a steam ferry boat. This project failing to pan out successfully the steam ferry enterprise was abandoned together with the charter, and subsequently, in May, 1857, a flatboat ferry was established by Isaac Parrish.

During the summer of 1855 thirty hewn log houses were built in the town, and business prospects were encouraging. Dr. A. Phinny, was the proprietor of the first store, and Charles Seltz who came down the Missouri in a skiff from the mountains, and stopped at DeSoto in the fall of 1855, was probably the second merchant to locate in the town. Harrison Critz, and Z. Jackson, each established a boarding house that year, and P. C. Sullivan was appointed postmaster.

In 1856 Levi and Marsh Kennard (both now residents of Omaha) established themselves in the mercantile line at De Soto, under the firm name of Kennard Bros. Thos. P. Kennard, now of Lincoln, is also one of the early settlers of the town, where he practiced law and, later, kept a hotel.

In 1857, a Mr. Fake, from Chicago, brought a heavy stock of liquors to De Soto, Samuel Francis establisded a hotel and the bank of De Soto entered upon a career of brilliant, but rather short-lived prosperity, with

Samuel Hall as president, Geo. E. Scott, cashier. In the same year the Waubeck Bank was established with H. H. Hine, president, and A. Castetter, teller, the latter doing all the business, and in the following spring the Corn Exchange bank was established by a Chicago firm, with J. Tucker as teller. Town property increased in price at a rapid rate, and the old settlers point with pride to the fact that a Mrs. Johnson refused $1,500 in gold for a certain corner lot. In 1857, the town had ten or a dozen saloons, nearly as many stores and a population of between six and seven hundred. Prosperity attended the settlers until the Pikes Peak and Cherry Creek gold excitement in the fall of 1857, when a majority of them abandoned the town and journeyed to the newly discovered gold fields.

Of course DeSoto had a "claim club" in those early days, in order to protect the first settlers in their land claims, and prevent their being taken away by later arrivals with more money, who came in before the land came into market. However, the club had no serious difficulty with any one, and when there was no longer any necessity for the organization it was allowed to die out.

The first minister who ever preached regularly at De Soto, was Rev. Jacob Adriance, of the Methodist Church. This was in 1857, services being held in a building which belonged to W. W. Wyman, then a resident of Omaha, where he edited the Omaha *Times*, and was afterwards postmaster at Omaha. He was father of the present Treasurer of the United States. It was in 1857 that Judge Wakely, Territorial Judge, Roger T. Beall and E. A. Allen, located in De Soto; Judge Wakely's family arriving in the fall.

The first sermon preached in the town, was in the fall of 1855, by a strange old character who wandered in one day, announced himself as a minister and asked for a room in which to hold religious services. A room was furnished him by Harrison Critz, proprietor of a boarding house, and it is remembered to this day, that the old man prayed that "this people may not become as barbarous as other heathen," to which the crowd present responded, "Amen!" Another wandering preacher was preaching there somewhat later to a congregation which filled the room full to overflowing, when a party of rowdys vented their disappointment at not being able to gain admittance by knocking the minister over his improvised pulpit, by throwing a dead dog at him.

In the fall of 1859, a young man was arrested on suspicion of being a member of a band of horse-thieves, which operated extensively in the vicinity, and was known to have its headquarters in or about the town. The young fellow "squealed" on condition he be released, and disclosed the whereabouts—in an old cave—of regularly drawn articles of organization, signed by the band, together with other valuable documents. The names of men standing high in the settlement and never before suspected, were found attached to these papers, and in consequence of their discovery, quite number of De Soto's leading citizens immediately decamped, and the band of horse-thieves was effectually broken up, though not until several arrests had been made.

A mile or two below De Soto, the Mormons made a settlement in 1846, after having been driven out of Nauvoo, Ill., and remained several years. Here were found well burned brick, in considerable quantities, by the first settlers of De Soto, which brick were used in walling up wells. Brigham Young occupied quarters one winter on the ground on which the De Soto flouring mill was built a few years ago.

Among the early settlers of the town, were the following: Judge Jessie T. Davis and family, Harrison Critz and family, Hugh McNeeley and family, Geo. McKinney and family, Sam Lewis, Z. Jackson, Potter C. Sullivan and family, Ephriam Sullivan and family, David McDonald and family, Porter S. Walker, Stephen Cass and family, James E. Smith and family, Z. Meekam and family, George W. Marlin and family, Z. S. Martin and family, Jeremiah Barnhart, Michael Tobey, T. M. Carter, (for whom Carter's Creek was named), Aleck Carter, Jr., Elisha P. Stout, Edward and Edwin Hayes, J. Bliss, Jacob Hill, J. T. McGiddagan, A. Phinney, Henry Way, Wm. Clancy, Jerry Sullivan, Charles Seltz, Roger T. Beall, E. N. Grennell, Geo. E. Scott and family, Samuel Francis and family, E. A. Allen, (now of Omaha,) Leroy and Lewis Tucker, with their families, Frank Goodwill and family, P. H. Knapp and family, Charles Powell, (now a member of the Board of Education at Omaha,) and family, Dr. Cutts and family, Con Orem, (who afterward became a noted pugalist in Colorado), A. Castetter and family, J. Tucker, J. W. Damon, Thos. R. Wilson, G. W. Wilson, M. V. Wilson, Soloman Himeline, George Obhurst, J. P. Ames, Constant Cacheline and family, Louis Bouvier and family. Dr. John Glover and family, W. H. B Stout, (now of Lincoln,) David Stout, Ferdinand Bujou and family, Joseph Buga and family, Geo. McKenzie and family, and John Carrigan and family.

The first district school house was built in 1860, and was 22x40 feet. There had been schools taught in the town previous to this date; however.

The lawyers who have located at De Soto and flung their shingles to the breeze, up to date, are: P. C. Sullivan, Charles D. Davis, Thomas P. Kennard, Roger T. Beall, Jessie T. Davis, John Carrigan and W. W Foote. The doctors are: Dr. — Cutts, Dr. — McLaughlin, Dr. John Glover, Dr. — Cannon, Dr. Charles Emerson Tennent, Dr. F.H.Longey, and Dr. S. H. Fawcett.

In 1856, Isaac Parrish, an ex-Congressman from Ohio, came to De Soto and "jumped" the western portion of the town site, building and occupying a claim shanty. The claim club called upon him and asked for an explanation, whereupon he agreed to give up his claim, provided he was allowed to put in a ferry across the Missouri opposite the town, which proposition was agreed to. Parish then jumped a portion of a town site called Cincinnati, on the opposite side of the river, at Shingle Point.

The first child born in De Soto, and probably the first in the county, was John Critz, born in June 1855. The first marriage was that of Thos. M. Carter and Miss Sullivan, sister of Poter C. Sullivan, the bride being but fourteen years of age at the time.

BLAIR.

A FLOURISHING LITTLE CITY.—FACTS AND FIGURES SHOWING ITS PROGRESS.

Blair can very properly be referred to as a "magic city." It was laid out in 1869, the first lots being sold on the 10th of March of that year, at auction. The town was located by John I. Blair and associates, members of the Sioux City and Pacific railroad company. The deeds to purchasers of lots came from John I. Blair and wife through W. W. Walker "attorney-in-fact" until about two years ago, since which they have been signed by "The Nebraska Town Company." At the first sale lots to the amount of over $100,000 were disposed of, and the town built up during the summer and fall of 1869 with remarkable rapidity. Its growth since has not been so rapid, but its prosperity has been unchecked, and the increase in population has been steady and continuous. The residents of the place have shown rare judgment and forethought in the planting of trees along the streets and about their grounds, and five years from this time Blair will be one of the most attractive towns in the State. The railroad company set a good example in the matter of tree planting, having, in the first settlement of the place, themselves planted out a handsome little park directly in front of their depot. These trees are now so large that the park was used last Fourth of July for the ceremonies of the day, which were attended by hundreds from all parts of the country. The Fourth of July, 1870, was also generally celebrated at Blair by the residents of the county. Then the public exercises were held in the pavillion of a circus which happened to be in the town. The oration was delivered by Judge John S. Bowen, and the celebration was a very pleasant affair indeed.

The first business house established in Blair was that of Herman Bros., dry goods, and the next that of Clark & Donovan, dealers in groceries and hardware, who afterwards sold out to John J. Adams. Among other business men who located at Blair at an early day, and are now doing business there, are West & Lewis, dry goods; Rosa & McBride, dry goods; J. H. Post, drugs; Haller & Lane, drugs; John Zerung—afterwards Peterson & Zerung—drugs; Smith & Dexter, dry goods; Martin Gallagher, furniture; Mathewson & Logan, dry goods and groceries; Palmer & Co., dry goods and groceries; M. C. Huyett, clothing; H. McBride, dry goods and groceries; Haller Bros., dry goods and groceries; William Maher, dry goods and groceries; R. W. Dawson, groceries; Wm. McCormick, groceries; E. Frederick, dry goods and groceries; H. C. Riordan—then Riordan & Kenney, and now Kenney & Stewart, hardware; Gus. Lunt, hardware; Graves & Frederick, agricultural implements; Chas. Shesrig, bakery, J. Nestal, bakery; A. Casper, bakery; M. Johnson, R. Waldo & Son, John Miller,——Lewis, Valentine Ganz, boots and shoes; M. C. Huyett & Co., Denney & Wild, Elam Clark & Son, James Foley, Kenney & Stewart, A. M. Crowdy, C. H. Eggleson, Foley & Lippincott, and E. M. Demmy, agricultural implements; Miss Lantry, Miss W. C. Walton, Mrs. McKay, Mrs. Hiiton, Mrs. Sarah E. Hidley, and Mrs. R. W. Dawson, millinery, Hotels have been established and kept by the following named persons: Keiley Bros., Martin Kloos, Wm. Maher, Wm. Carson, Mrs. A. M. Quimby, Mrs. E. E. Sketchley, George Seik, and Henry Seurt. Levy & Chapman, ——Hammersling, and John Connell have been or are now engaged in dealing in harness. Butcher shops have been kept or are still kept by Sheeley & Irvy, Wm. O'Hara, Wm. Miller, J. C. Hart, M. V. Wilson, John Connell, Bowen & Parks, J. G. Smith, and John Parks. Grain dealers, Elam Clark & Son, C. C. Crowell, and the Blair City Mill Co. Blacksmiths, John Tew, Frank Stanford, Ed. Cochrane, and John H. Smith. Physicians, F. H. Longley, S. B. Taylor, S. H. Fawcett, C. Emerson Tennant, ——— McLean, D. H. O'Linn, Wm. H. Palmer. Lawyers, Davis & Carrigan—now Carrigan and Osborne—W. C. Walton, B. F. Hilton, J. S. Bowen, M. Ballard, A. D. Brainard, and S. H. Tucker. Real estate agents, Alex. Reed, Alonzo Perkins, A. Castetter. Banker, A. Castetter.

The Blair City mill, which was completed recently, is doing a fine business. It is owned by H. B. Dexter, Eli H. Turton, V. G. Lantry, T. M. Carter, and Mr. Wortendyke.

Dr. S. H. Fawcett is postmaster, with Harry M. Bowen as assistant.

The assessed valuation of real estate, for taxable purposes was, last year $116,005; personal property $60,390. The amount received from taxes and licenses for 1875 was $3,555.62. The liquor license is $500 per annum, and the result is the town is not overrun with low droggeries. The license on theatrical exhibitions, circuses, etc., is from three to twenty-five dollars.

The newspapers of Blair are referred to in preceeding pages.

The town of Blair was first under control of a board of trustees appointed by the county commissioners, and consisted of the following named:

1869—J. H. Post, chairman, Alex Reed, Dr. F. H. Longley, C. B. Herman, M. V. Wilson.

1870—Dr. S. W. Fawcett, chairman, J. D. Kieley, A. T. Chapin, John Ayer, Dr. S. B. Taylor, Alex Reed, John Carrigan, attorney.

1871—J. H. Hungate chairman, A. F. Chapin, J. H. Kimball, Peter Seih, Dr. S, B. Taylor.

1872—L. W. Osborne chairman. J. H. Hungate, Peter Seih, J. H. Kimball, W. C. Walton.

In September, 1872, the town was organized as a city of the second-class, and the following named were elected:

J. H. Hungate mayor, Wm. Maher, E. M. Denny, John W. Tew, Mike Gallagher, councilmen; Jno. S. Bowen, police judge; Rice Arnold, city marshal.

1873—C. C. Crowell, mayor; E. M. Denny, Mike Gallagher. Wm. Maher, W. C. Walton, councilmen; Jesse T. Davis, police judge; Thomas S. Heck, clerk; Joe Fox, city marshal.

1874—Dr. W. H. Palmer, mayor; E. M. Denny, F. H. Matthisen, Dr. D. H. O'Linn, W. D. Gross, councilmen; Jesse T. Davis, police judge; Thomas Heck, clerk; Joe Fox, marshal.

1875—J. H. Hungate, mayor; Dr. D. H. O'Linn, W. D. Gross, Dr. W. H. Palmer, Henry Collins, councilmen; A. Rockwell, clerk and police judge; Alex Reed, treasurer, Joe Fox, city marshal.

1876—F. W. Kenny, mayor; O. V. Palmer, W. D. Gross, H. C. Graves, E. Cacheline, councilmen; A. Rockwell, police judge; E. M. Denny, clerk; Alex Reed, treasurer; H. L. Fisher, marshal.

The Blair High School building, erected in 1872 at a cost of $15,000, is one of the finest in the state; and with its efficient corps of teachers is fast acquiring reputation as a first-class institution of learning.

Last year over $300,00 was used in shipping hogs and cattle from Blair by regular dealers, distributed about as follows:

James Foley, $100,000; W. W. McKinney, $50,000; Herman Bros., $60,000; J. P. & W. W. Latta, $50,000; Iowa parties, $25,000; O. Dodson, $20,000; G. W. Wilson, $15,000. In addition to this, A. S. Warrick, Charles Blackstone, R. Blasco, Joseph Johnson, Wm. Hilgenkamp, and other farmers shipped stock extensively on their own account, which would make the total amount of money used in this business during the season, probably $400,000.

The building used for a court house was erected for school purposes by a firm of contractors in Blair, as a private speculation. The school authorities did not conclude to purchase the building, however, and it was sold to the county. In it are located the offices of the county treasurer and clerk, a hall on the second floor being used for court purposes. The finances of the county have been ably managed, as a general thing, and, as it is one of the wealthiest and most prosperous counties in the State, a suitable and commodious court house is doubtless a thing of the near future. One bill of expense, to which the county has been subjected, has arisen from three or four protracted murder trials, in each of which cases there has been disagreements by the jury, necessitating a second hearing. The expense of the Randall trial alone was about $5,000—a sum sufficient to pay court expenses for two years, under ordinary circumstances.

The county jail is located several squares from the court house, and is, perhaps, less suited for jail purposes than any similar structure on the face of the earth, being small, inconveniently arranged, and the cells damp and unhealthly. It was built soon after the county seat was located at Blair, and cost some $8,000. For this sum an excellent jail building, large enough to supply the wants of the county for half a century, could now be built. It seems to be an absolute necessity, however, that counties in the west should pay for some very expensive lessons, and Washington county in comparison with some of her neighbors, has passed through this experience at a moderate outlay.

CUMING CITY.

ONE OF THE OLDEST TOWNS IN THE STATE—A COLLEGE WHICH HAS NO GRADUATES—A BRACE OF ANCIENT NEWSPAPERS—A TERRIBLE SCARE.

The following sketch of Cuming City, is taken from the the very interesting historical address of Mr. Perry Selden, delivered at Blair, July 4th, of the present year:

"Cuming City, one of the ancient cities of Washington county, was "claimed" by P. G. Cooper and two others, in September, 1854. No settlement was made, however, until the spring of 1855, when actual settlers early made their appearance, in sufficient numbers to justify the project of a city. Accordingly a "site" was located, mapped, surveyed, and named in honor of the Acting Governor, T. B. Cuming. It is claimed that the election for Burt county, in December, 1854, was held near Cuming City, on South creek; while others claim for that honor, a position in the willows, on the bank of the Missouri River, near De Soto. The later is, no doubt, the most valid claim, as the parties to that election came up from Omaha on the day of voting, and were not likely, under the circumstances, to go farther than across the imaginary line, which was at that time between De Soto and Fort Calhoun. Be this as it may, certain it is, that the regular election at Cuming City, in November, 1855, was held under a cottonwood tree, near the present bridge on South creek.

"Flattered and encouraged with the patronage of territorial officials Cuming City soon became a place of importance and great future prospects. The inevitable ferry charter was granted to P. G. Cooper in January, 1856, by the legislature, and the same month "Washington College" was incorporated and located at Cuming City, and the same act appointed a board of Trustees consisting of the following distinguished persons, viz: R. R. Folsom, James Mitchell, T. B. Cuming, Mark W. Izard, P. G. Cooper, William B. Hall, John C. Campbell and J. B. Radford.

" In 1857 the Nebraska *Pioneer*, a weekly newspaper was started under the management of a man named Dimmick. At the election in November, 1856, one of the representative men of Cuming City and an early settler, Mr. James S. Stewart, was chosen as a representative, together with E. P. Stout and William Connor; while William Clancy was elected councilman.

" In 1857 there was in Cuming City, fifty-three dwecling houses, three stores, three hotels, besides several boarding houses and a number of saloons. At the election this year Cuming City was again honored by the selection of two of its prominent citizens as representatives: Mr. James

S. Stewart was re-elected with P. G. Cooper of Cuming City, and Alonzo Perkins, of De Soto, as colleagues.

"In 1858 came into existence, and flourished for a while, the Cuming City *Star*, a weekly newspaper conducted by L. M. Kline. In November 1858, by act of the legislature, the "Cuming City Ferry Company" was incorporated, and by the same act the former charter granted to P. G. Cooper, was revoked. This ferry company consisted of P. G. Cooper, L. M. Kline. George A. Brigham, and others.

"The first general fourth of July celebration in Washington county occurred at the grove on North Creek, near Cuming City, in 1860. Almost the entire population of the county was in attendance. Judge John S. Bowen was the orator of the day, and the Declaration of Independence was read by Alman Bender. A band from Tekamah was in attendance, and altogether the affair was a grand success without precedent or parallel in the history of the county. Cuming City at this time was more flourishing and populous than at any more recent date Although it continued a place of some importance, yet the zenith of its glory had been reached and for the ensuing nine years there was no perceptible change."

It was at this celebration that a newly wedded wife came near being abandonded by her husband. Among those present was a Methodist preacher by the name of Turman, who was stationed at Fontenelle that year, and was known far and near for his eccentricities. He had married recently to the astonishment of all his acquaintances and to his own also, no doubt, and he and Mrs. Turman both attended this fourth of July celebration. As the people were leaving the grove in the evening, after the festivities of the day, some one in the wagon in which Furman was riding, suddenly turned to him with the inquiry: "Why, Mr. Turman, where's your wife?" "Sure enough," exclaimed the absent-minded preacher, as he jumped from the wagon to return to the grove,"I knew I had forgotten something," and he ran back in search of his missing rib.

Among the first setttlers of Cuming City may be mentioned Jacob Pate, Lorenzo Pate, J. Zimmerman, J. Gall, E. Pilcher, P. G. Cooper, J. S. Stewart, L. M. Kline, T. C. Hungate, O. W. Thomas, Geo. A. Brigham, A. W. Merrick, L. R. Fletcher, Giles Mead, J. C. Lippincott, J. Boice, J. Johnson.

In the fall of 1876 the Cuming City timber claim was jumped by some Irishmen. A large party, armed with guns, ropes and all the "necessaries" went down to the shanty occupied by the intruders for the purpose of forcing them to terms. They tore down the shanty and, not finding the larger "game" they expected, began shooting birds for pastime. Some of the party had been left in the rear to take care of the teams and they hearing the firing, supposed hostilities on a scale of unexpected magnitude had commenced,and so fled to town in hot haste, taking the teams with them and giving the women folks who had assembled on Fish creek a terrible fright. An hour later their anxiety was relieved by the remainder of the party straggling in afoot and reporting nobody hurt. In the following spring the Irishmen were drowned in the big flood, and Cuming City secured her timber claim.

HERMAN.

A Five Year Old Town That Has Built Up Rapidly.

The town of Herman was laid out in 1871, on a tract of land owned by the Omaha and Northwestern railroad company, James G. Megeath, and T. W. T. Richards, and named in honor of Samuel Herman, who has occupied the position of conductor on the Omaha and Northwestern since it was put in operation. The new town soon became an important shipping point for stock and grain as it has been the terminus of the railroad up to this time, though at the present writing, July 28, 1876, it is being rapidly pushed through to Tekamah, the county seat of Burt county.

Dock Kimball was the first agent of the railroad at Herman, and was the first to engage in mercantile business there, in which he was quite succesful. At this time the grangers own and operate a grain elevator at Herman, as do also Elam Clark & son. J. J. Stubbs, formerly assistant engineer on the Omaha and Northwestern, is an extensive grain dealer and so is W. W. Darrell, who is also engaged in general merchandizing. W. S. Richards is the postmaster and he, too keeps a large stock of dry goods, groceries, boots and shoes, etc. John Bradford sells groceries, dry goods and hardware; W. R. Fitch does the blacksmithing for the residents of that section of the country, and L. Davis supplies the travelling public with livery and buys and sells stock.

The town is surrounded by a splendid country for farming and stock raising, and is being rapidly settled up. It is the only town between Blair and Tekamah, and is destined to become an important point. Lots now sell at prices varying from twenty-five to one hundred and fifty dollars.

HUDSON.

A Paper Town, Better Known in the East Than to Its Next Door Neighbors.

There are a great many residents of Washington county who never knew—and probably would have gone down to the silent tomb without the knowledge, but for this veracious chronicle of the past—that in 1856 a very enterprising citizen of the wooden nutmeg State, one W. E. Walker, was the sole owner and proprietor of a town site in a swamp in the extreme northeast corner of the county, which town site he christened Hudson. More than this: He platted another town site in a like eligible locality immediately opposite, on the Iowa side of the Missouri, called it Melrose, published beautiful lithograps by the hundreds, representing the two towns, with busy steamers plying between them endeavoring to supply transportation for the enormous traffic constantly carried on between the two towns. Armed with these, aided and abetted by a tongue remarkable for the oily rapidity with which it could be manipulated, Walker meandered up and down the eastern states, engaged in lecturing, and, at the close of each lecture, would sell off lots in Hudson and Melrose, at the rate of one dollar each, with astonishing rapidity. A plat of Hudson can be seen at the office of County Clerk Jackson, and this plat shows that the town was comprised of 8,720 lots, consisting of fifty blocks, 2,000 feet long by 200 wide, four blocks of the same length, 100 feet wide, ten blocks 2,250 feet long by 200 in width, and one block of the length last given by 100 feet in width. The streets were from 45 to 60 feet wide, and there was not an alley in the town. The sale of lots in Hudson was so great for the first few years after its location, that the county clerks accumulated considerable weath by recording the deeds therefor at the rate of one dollar each. The deeds were printed, the name of Walker being also printed, so that when lots were sold all he had to do was to insert the name of the purchaser and number of lots purchased. The deeds poured into the county clerk's office from all over the east, and it is estimated that Walker made at least $5,000 by his scheme. To this day county officials are bothered with letters from eastern suckers inquiring as to the present price of lots in Hudson, and the writer was shown recently a batch of thirteen deeds, which had been sent in one envelope from Chicago, to be recorded.

GRANT, SHERIDAN AND LINCOLN PRECINCTS.

SOME FACTS CONCERNING THE MORE RECENT SETTLED PORTIONS OF THE COUNTY.

The above named precincts are of comparatively recent settlement; but wonderful changes have been wrought within their boundaries during the past half dozen years.

Grant precinct is in the northern part of the county, west of Herman. Among its first settlers were L. H. Thone, Martin Peterson, Gilbert Thone, Wm. Ravers, L. D. Cameron, Foxwell Fletcher, Edward Fletcher, S. C. Rose, Perry Selden, Frank Whizinand, Mr. Crane, Josiah Pace, Alfred Van Valen, Samuel Spiker, Thomas Wilson, M. P. Preston, Mr. Geary. Most of these men have now splendid farms, and are more or less engaged in stock raising. The precinct is well watered by New York creek and its tributaries, along which are beautiful valleys specially adapted to grazing, the grass growing rich and luxuriant.

Sheridan precinct extends to the western border of the county, on the north. Its first settlements were made along Clark creek in 1856-'7, when that portion of the county belonged to Dodge county, though the interior and eastern portions of the precinct were not settled until many years later. Among the Clark and Logan creek settlers were Chris. Leiser, Charles and Fred Eisley, Uriah Thomas, Harvey J. Robinson, (who built the first grist mill on the fine water power now owned and occupied by A. C. Briggs & Son,) John and Silas Seeley, Sam'l Williams, Tom and Sam. Parks, Sullivan Gaylord, J. B. Robinson, John and Dick Shur; (the former was accidently shot and killed by Tom Parks during the Indian scare of 1859); John Cayton and his father in-law Mr. Clark, Chris. Hinneman and Mr. McBroom. At one time there was a postoffice on Clark creek called Lewisburg, but it was sacked by the Pawnees in June 1859, and discontinued soon after. The following named have located in the precinct within the past ten years: W. A. Johnson, Phillip Gozzard, David Clark and his son, Hiram G. Clark, (who have this year nearly 600 head of sheep, quite a number of cattle and hogs, barns costing $2,000, and a farm of 720 acres, on which they are raising 250 acres of corn in one field,) Archie Bouver, O. H. Hatch, Robert Adams, John Adams, Anson Hewitt, C. B. Sprague, Robert Schenk, Frank Hancock, J. M. Jackson,

Joseph Cook, Henry E. Meservey, Mr. Arnold, Mathew Maloney, Thomas Dunn.

Lincoln precinct was organized about ten years ago. The first movement towards obtaining proprietory possession of land in this precinct was made in the year 1856, by Pomery Searle on a portion of the farm now owned and occupied by E. G. Gaylord, (our present State representative.) The following year Searle broke about 20 acres and set a portion in fruit and forest trees. In 1858 he went to California, and the first permanent improvement was made in 1868 by the present occupant. Eight years ago there were but two families living on the route from Cuming City to Fontenelle, viz: A. Southerland and Benjamin Taylor. F. Curtis had his cabin up, but it was unoccupied. On the north, to the line of Burt county, there were only four settlers. There were a few settlements on the southern border of the precinct.

In the year 1857, John Mattes pre-empted the place now owned by William Hilgenkamp, and the following year a Mr. Coyle settled on the adjoining place north, now owned by William's father. With the exception of Mr. Parker, who settled on the place now owned by Herman Stork, there was no new settlements made in the precinct until about 1862. Wm. Hilgenkamp bought of John Mattes, has added to and improved until he has a farm ranked among the best in the county. James R. Thorp bought the land he now owns among the early purchases, but went I think, to California and China, returning to his old home in the State of New York in time to enlist and go through the war of the Rebellion, after which, he returned and located on his place in the year 1868.

In 1865 or 1866, the influx of Homesteaders commenced, and settlements were made by Geo. Morley, Frank Curtis and John B. Young and sons, followed soon after by H. N. Mattison, his son George, Mr. Ostrander, Mr. Jenson, Henry Hilgenkamp, Peter Hilgenkamp, and others who have secured good farms and are making the wild prairies teem with fields of grain, fruit and forest trees.

In 1857, Wm. R. Hamilton, (county commissioner for six years past), and W. M. Saint, settled on the west side of Bell creek. In the fall of the same year, a party of nine Indians made a raid upon Saint's cabin, (he being absent at the time), robbed it of all the provisions, cut open the feather bed, gave its contents to the wind, replaced the same with the stolen property, secured it upon a pony, and then mounting, raised a whoop, and charged upon Mr. Hamilton and his brother-in-law, who were building a sod stable at his place, and who stood upon the defensive, arms in hand. After circling around them awhile in a menancing manner, and finding they "didn't scare worth a cent," the red skins came to a parly, and wanted something to eat. Upon being refused, they made a break for the house, but were beaten in the race by Mr. Hamilton who finally drove them off. On the following day, Mr. Hamilton and Mr. Saint went to the Indian camp, on the west side of the Elkhorn river, to try to recover the stolen property, but were unsuccessful.

The spring of 1858 opened with a scarcity of provisions among the pioneers, and Mr. Hamilton with a team of three yoke of oxen, started in search of supplies, and in the course of his travels found himself at Magnolia, Harrison county, Iowa, having crossed the Missouri river on the ice. After obtaining the needed supplies and starting for home, he was told that the crossing was unsafe, but there was no alternative. The family at home were in need and the stream must be crossed at all hazards, so locking the wheel of his wagon, drove down the bank upon the ice. While trying to undo the lock, the ice sank about eighteen inches; he not wishing to travel in that direction, whipped up his team and came over in safety.

FONTENELLE.

[handwritten: Thomas Keller was elected president and on the town site. [J. Waller]]

One of the Oldest Towns in the State—The Catfish War—Sinking of the Steamer Mary Cole—Church Organization—Death of Logan Fontenelle.

In the year 1854, a company was organized at Quincy, Illinois, for the purpose of securing to its members and their families homes in the new Territory of Nebraska. The company was called "The Nebraska Colinization Company," though as to whether or not it proposed "colonizing" the entire area of Nebraska, tradition is silent. Certain it is, however, that in July of that year, Rev. W. W. Keep, Jonathan Smith, J. W. Richardson, Jared Blanset, C. Bernard, William Flach and James A. Bell, (father of the writer), came to Nebraska in order to "view the land," and locate the colony on behalf of the company. They crossed Iowa in wagons—as there was not then a foot of railroad track west of the Mississippi—camping out on the way, and in due time reached the embryo city of Omaha, which had just been laid out by the Nebraska & Council Bluffs Steam Ferry Company. There is a legend to the effect that this latter company, becoming alarmed at the advent of the Quincy chaps and their contemplated rival town, offered them a one-third interest in the townsite of Omaha, if they would stop there and not locate a rival city. This offer was rejected—promptly and unanimously rejected—as our company from the Sucker State desired an entire town of their own, and were not to be turned aside from their purpose by the offer of one-third of a townsite which, at that time, had no advantages over a score of other localities.

Passing out beyond the bluffs of the Missouri and the tributaries to that stream, these Quincy pilgrims found a section of country which, for agricultural and grazing purposes, has no superior on this continent—or any other. Arriving in the vicinity of the Elkhorn, in their northwesterly course, they came to a stream of considerable size, over which it was necessary to throw a temporary bridge, in order to cross it. To do this, some one had to "coon it" across the stream on a log, and this task was undertaken by Mr. James A. Bell. Before reaching the other bank, however, he "heard something drop" into the stream below, and was surprised to find that it was himself. He was at once fished out and spread out on the grass to dry. In consequence of this little episode the party immediately christened the stream "Bell creek," which name it still bears. Crossing this stream, the colonizers pursued their way to the banks of the Elkhorn, and were so pleased with the surrounding country that they decided to locate there, and the town site of Fontenelle was laid out, claims made, etc., by the party, who then proceeded to the camp of the Omaha Indians—in honor of whose chief, Logan Fontenelle, the town was named—and held a grand pow-wow with the tribe for the purpose of securing its good will. They also paid Fontenelle the sum of ten dollars each, with the understanding that he was to protect their interests until members of the company could be sent out and established in their new town, and then returned to Quincy.

I am not able to give the names of the entire membership of the company, as it was organized in Quincy, but it included Jonathan Smith, President, Rev. W. W. Keep, Secretary, J. W. Richardson, J. C. Bernard, Treasurer; O. C. Bernard, H. Metz, John Evans, (now of Evans & Durnall, Omaha), J. Armor, H. G. Mauzey, E. M. Davis, W. H. Davis, Jared Blansett, G. Williamsons, J. McIntosh, Rufus Brown, —— Root and James A. Bell.

In the fall of 1854, the company sent out Judge J. W. Richardson as their agent, to occupy the town site, on behalf of the company. Judge Richardson was accompanied by his wife—now Mrs. Wm. Kline, and still a resident of Fontenelle. At Council Bluffs they were joined by Col. Wm. Kline and Col. Doyle, of South Carolina, who had recently been appointed Marshal for the new Territory. In November, Dr. M. H. Clark, was elected councilman, and Col. Doyle and Judge Richardson, representatives to the Territorial Legislature, from Dodge county, in which Fontenelle was then the only settlement. The colonization company at Quincy instructed their agent, Judge Richardson, to use every effort to secure the location of the Territorial capital at Fontenelle, and also dispatched two of their number—Smith and Bernard—to Omaha, to lobby in that interest during the session of the Legislature. Their efforts were in vain, however, and Omaha secured the prize. They succeeded, though, in securing a charter for a college to be located at Fontenelle; and to be run under Baptist auspices, a town charter and a ferry charter, the latter in favor of Col. Kline. The county of Dodge was organized and Fontenelle designated as the county seat thereof. During the session, a bill was introduced, chartering the Platte Valley and Pacific railroad company, and on the 16th of February, 1855, Dr. Clark, as chairman of the committee on corporations, submitted thereon a report of masterly ability, showing a clear understanding of existing facts and far-sighted grasp of the future of this great enterprise, from which report, I quote the following prediction. " In view of the wonderful changes that will result, your committee cannot believe the period remote when this work will be accomplished, and with liberal encouragement to capital which your committee are disposed to grant, it is their belief that before *fifteen years* have transpired, the route to India will be opened and the way across this continent will be the common highway of the world." Fourteen years and three months from that date, was driven the golden spike which completed this world's highway.

The erroneous idea prevailed among the founders of Fontenelle, that the Platte and Elkhorn rivers could be used for purposes of navigation, and that water communication could be established between Plattsmouth and Fontenelle. With this object in view, the company at Quincy secured a small steamer, of the ferry boat style, and a portion of them, with their families, embarked at Quincy on the steamer "Mary Cole," bound for Fontenelle. The trip was made safely, until near the mouth of the Platte river, where she was snagged and completely wrecked. The lives of the passengers were saved with difficulty, but the cargo was almost entirely lost. Among the passengers on board the boat, were Samuel Whittier, (now of Fremont), wife and daughter Mary; W. H. Davis and family; Henry Peters and family; J. McIntosh and family; Miss Henrietta Redner, now Mrs. John W. Pattison of Sedalia, Mo.; Miss Phœbe Bartup, afterwards Mrs. H. C. Lemon and Mike McDonald.

The first death in Fontenelle was that of two men who were killed by Indians, supposed to be a straggling party of Santee Sioux. One Saturday evening in July, 1855, a Mr. and Mrs. Porter, and young man named Demaree—the latter the son of a wealthy farmer living near Quincy, Illinois—came up from Bell Creek where they had been breaking prairie and encamped on Sam Francis' lake, a mile south of Fontenelle, intending to go up into the settlement Sunday morning. As they were about to leave camp Sunday, a party of Indians rode out of the willows and approached Porter's wagon. One of them snatched Demaree's hat off his head and was riding off with it, when the owner called to him to stop or he would shoot him, picking up his rifle as he spoke. The Indian turned, saw this demonstration on the part of Demaree called out "Pawnee!" and shot him instantly, the ball passing through Porter also, killing both men. The Indians then rode off, leaving Mrs. Porter alone with the dead. The horrified woman raised the head of her husband and vainly strove to restore him to consciousness. Failing in this effort she started for Fontenelle, perfectly frantic with fear and excitement, and the story she told upon her arrival led the settlers to believe they were in danger of being attacked by an overwhelming force of Indians at any moment. At that time the nearest white settlement was that of Omaha—forty miles distant—hence no outside assistance could be expected. Arrangements were hastily made to repulse the expected attack, but fortunately, none was made. The Indians who had caused the alarm returned to their own "range," many miles to the westward and were never again seen in that section.

In consequence of this double murder, many long and weary months were passed before the settlers considered themselves safe from assault and massacre by their red skin neighbors. The Governor of the Territory was implored to send out troops, and a militia company was sent out by him to Fontenelle and stationed there during the fall and winter.

T entire organization was called Beal's Rangers. The company from Omaha was under command of Captain William Moore as captain, with John Y. Clopper as first, and —— Hepburn as second lieutenant. The Fontenelle company was commanded by Captain Kline, Russell Mc-Neally being first lieutenant, and John W. Pattison second. The ladies of the colony having been deprived of religious services on Sunday for many months, after consultation, called at the camp of these warriors from abroad Sunday morning in order to see if some one of their number would not consent to lead in religious exercises; but, upon arriving at the building in which they were quartered, were completely discouraged upon discovering the invidual, whom they had all agreed was most likely to be the person to assume these duties, lying flat on his back, with his feet perched in the air, singing "Oh darkies, how my heart grows weary." The ladies backed out at once, without making known their mission.

In the fall of 1855 Thomas Gibson—now of the real estate firm of Schaller & Gibson, Omaha,—was elected at Fontenelle to represent Dodge county in the legislature.

In May, 1856, Rev. Reuben Gaylord, of Omaha, organized a Congregational church at Fontenelle, consisting of the following named: Samuel Strickland, Mrs. Emily K. Strickland, Miss Emily F. Strickland, Thomas Gibson, Mrs. Sarah Gibson, James H. Peters, Mrs. Jane Peters, Rev. Thomas Waller, Lucien Kennedy, Rufus Brown, Mrs. Nancy Brown, James A. Bell, Miss Mary Bell, Edward Corless, Miss Mary Corless, John Francis, Mrs. Maria Francis, Silas J. Francis, Mrs. Celestia Francis, Cyrus Howell, Edward Holmes, Mrs. Elvina Holmes, Wm. G. Bingham and Mrs. Lucy C. Bingham. Thomas Gibson and James A. Bell were elected deacons, and Rev. Thomas Waller was appointed the first pastor. The new church was presented with a handsome silver communion service by the First Congregational church of Quincy, Illinois. Since that time the following named have served as pastors of the church: Rev. E. B. Hurlbut, Rev. Wm. McCandlish, Rev. L. H. Jones, Rev. C. E. Bisbee, Rev. Isiah Smith, Rev. Thomas Douglas, Rev. Reuben Gaylord. A Sunday school was organized at the same time the church was.

In addition to those named above as joining the Congregational church, there were living at Fontenelle and in the vicinity, at that time or came in during the summer of 1856, the following: Judge and Mrs. Richardson, John W. Pattison, Chris. Leiser and family, Col. Kline, Samuel Whittier and family, Rev. J. M. Taggart—now of Palmyra, Neb.—and family, Miss Ellen Griffeth, Willis Carr, Eli, Harlow and Edward Carpenter, Isaac Underwood and family, Mrs. Denslow and family, B. L. Keyes and family, Wm. M. Saint, John Baty and family, John Evans and family, Rufus Brown and family, Henry Sprick, John K. Cramer and family, Ab. Yost, Wm. and Theodore Keep, Miss Caroline Davis, Wm. H. Davis and family, Christy Archilles and family, Morris Wogan and family, Arthur Bloomer, John Bloomer, David Bloomer,

Thomas Fitzsimmons and family, Sam. Francis and family, Wm. H. Johnson, Henry C. Lemon and family, George Hindley, Jared Blansett, Wm. Flach and family, Mr. Osterman and family, J. M. Hancock and family, Jacob Canaya and family, John Ray and family, Deacon Searle and family, John and Silas Seeley, Pomeroy Searle, Sam. Williams and family, Hiram Ladd and family, Sumner D. Prescott, Wm. R. Hamiiton and family, Henry Brinkman and family, Wm. Hecker Sr., Orlando and Pierce Himebaugh, Wm. C. Hecker, Julius Brainard and family—now of Blair.

In 1856 a college building was erected by the Congregationalists, to whom the Baptists has assigned their charter. A flourishing school was kept up for a number of years, Prof. Burt being the first teacher, and the building was used for lyceums and all kinds of public meetings, the first settlers of Fontenelle being an eminently sociable people. Annual festivals, with bounteous suppers, were held in the college building about New Year's day, until about the close of the war, to which festivals the settlers, for many miles around, came regularly, bringing well laden baskets, and when the contents of these baskets were distributed and arranged on the long tables, the only reason the latter didn't groan was because they were not of the groaning kind.

In the summer of 1856, a Methodist church was organized by Rev. Jerome Spillman—now of Atlanta, Georgia,—and, in 1863, a Presbyterian church was organized by Rev. Wm. McCandlish, who settled in Fontenelle in 1858, and is now agent for the American Bible Society for Nebraska, Wyoming and Colorado. The Lutherans organized a church about the same time, with Rev. J. F. Kuhlman,—now residing at Ponca City, Neb.,—as their first pastor.

The Pawnee war of 1859, described at length in preceding pages, was a serious detriment to the settlers of Fontenelle. When the Indians first came over from their villages on the Platte, they pillaged extensively from the citizens. While thus engaged, parties of a dozen or more were driven from their respective premises, by Mrs. Kline and Mrs. Hiram Ladd. In coming down from West Point, after the killing of the Indians there, Wm. H. Johnson, Henry Sprick, Wm. C. Hecker and Mr. Artman became detached from the rest of the party, and were compelled to foot it to Fontenelle, distant some thirty miles. They avoided the road, and, as they traveled cautiously over the wild prairie, thought they saw a party of savages in the distance, and at once took refuge in a slough, where they remained in the water and grass until dark. Upon reaching Fontenelle, they learned that the party they had mistaken for Indians were white men.

In March, 1857, a Mr. Martin, of Fremont, was drowned in attempting to ford the Elkhorn at Fontenelle, and on the 5th of July, 1867, a terrible accident befell the families of Rev. O. C. Dake and John Ray, of Fremont. They were returning home from Fontenelle, where they had been spending the Fourth, when, in crossing the Elkhorn in the flat boat ferry, their wagon was backed off into the river by the restive horses.

The water proved to be only waist deep, but in consequence of a belief that it was much deeper—Messes Dake and Ray being unable to swim—two of Mr. Dake's and three of Mr. Ray's children were drowned.

In the winter of 1858-'9 Fontenelle became a part of Washington county in consequence of a reorganization of the county lines.

The first school was taught in the winter of 1855-6 by Miss Emily Strickland, the next by Wm. M. Saint, and the third by Pomeroy Searle.

The first stock of goods was brought to the new settlement in 1855 by Wm. H. Davis, who also kept the first hotel—a double log house called the Fontenelle House. He was bought out by J. M. Hancock, in 1856.

The first child born in the town was Mattie Francis, daughter of Samuel Francis—October 2d, 1855. A few hours later, the same night, a daughter was born to Mr. and Mrs. Wm. H. Davis, and named Fontenella. The town company had promised a town lot to the parents of the first child born in the town, and consequently the first birth was a matter of general interest. It is said that one good lady, who had a child born a day or two after those mentioned above, consoled her somewhat disappointed family with the remark: "Well, never mind, papa is able to buy town lots for his children."

By Thomas Waller

The first marriage that occurred at Fontenelle was that of Henry Whittier and Miss Emily Strickland, in the fall of 1856. Harlow Carpenter and Miss Ellen Griffith were married during the following winter. Also that fall there were a couple of runaway matches, the parties being married under a cedar tree on the banks of the Elkhorn in a driving rain, by Rev. Silas J. Francis. The parties were Frank Fox, and Miss Harriet Whittier, and John W. Pattison and Miss Henrietta Redner.

In the summer of 1855, Harlow Carpenter, John Cramer, Isaac Underwood, and others, commenced the manufacture of brick, but their labors were suspended by the "catfish war," of that summer, after they had about ten thousand brick ready for the kiln. The next summer John Ray burned a large kiln.

The first saw mill was erected by Samuel and Silas Francis, in the summer of 1856. They sold it that fall to Wm. H. Johnson and Henry C. Lemon.

Perhaps I cannot close my sketch of the first settlement of Fontenelle better than by giving the following interesting account of the death and burial of the man after whom it is named, which account I take from S. T. Bangs' centennial history of Sarpy county:

"Logan Fontenelle was a half breed, his father being French. He was educated in St. Louis; spoke English fluently, and was at this time about thirty years of age, of medium height, swarthy complexion, black hair and dark piercing eyes. In the middle of the summer of 1855 a procession might have been seen wending its way towards the old home of Logan Fontenelle on the bluffs overlooking the Missouri river and above the stone quarries at Bellvue. It moved slowly along led by Louis Sansosee, who was driving a team with a wagon in which, wrapped in blankets and buffalo robes, was all that was mortal of Logan Fontenelle, the chief of the Omahas. On either side the Indian chiefs and braves mounted on ponies, with the squaws and relatives of the deceased, expressed their grief in mournful outcries. His remains were taken to the house which he had left a short time before, and now, desolate and afflicted, they related the incidents of his death. He had been killed by the Sioux on the Loup Fork thirteen days before, while on a hunt with the Omahas. Having left the main body with San-so-see in pursuit of game, and while in a ravine that hid them from the sight of the Omahas, they came in contact with a band of Sioux on the war-path, who attacked them. San-so-see escaped in some thick underbrush while Fontenelle stood his ground, fighting desperately and killing three of his adversaries, when he fell, pierced with fourteen arrows, and the prized scalp-lock was taked by his enemies. The Omahas did not recover his body until the next day.

"It was the wish of Col. Sarpy to have him interred on the bluffs, fronting the house in which he had lived, and a coffin was made which proved too small without unfolding the blankets which enveloped him, and as he had been dead so long, this was a disagreeabe task. After putting him in the coffin, his wives who witnessed the scene uttered the most piteous cries, cutting their ankles until the blood ran in streams. An old Indian woman who looked like the witch of Endor, standing between the house and the grave, lifted her arms to Heaven and shrieked her maledictions upon the heads of his murderers. Colonel Sarpy, Stephen Decatur, Mrs. Sloan, an Otoe half breed and others stood over the grave where his body was being lowered, and while Decatur was reading the impressive funeral service of the Episcopal church, he was interrupted by Mrs. Sloan, who stood by his side and in a loud tone told him that 'a man of his character ought to be ashamed of himself to make a mockery of the Christian religion by reading the solemn services of the church.' He proceeded, however, until the end. After the whites, headed by Col. Sarpy, had paid their last respects, the Indians filed around the grave, and made a few demonstrations of sorrow; the whites dispersing to their homes, and the Indians to relate their own exploits and the daring of their dead chief."

BELL CREEK.

AN ENTERPRISING TOWN ON THE SIOUX CITY & PACIFIC—A GRATIFYING EXHIBIT OF WHAT HAS BEEN ACCOMPLISHED IN SIX YEARS.

One of the most enterprising railroad towns in the county, is that of Bell Creek, situated on the Sioux City & Pacific railroad, on a beautiful stretch of table land, between the Elkhorn river and the creek after which the town was named. It was laid out by the railroad company in 1869, the company having purchased 120 acres from a Mr. Carter, 160 from John Gannon, and 160 from another party, for town purposes. Only a portion of this land was platted, however, the remainder being held as a "reserve" for further use. The lots are 60 by 140 feet, divided at right angles by streets eighty and alleys twenty feet wide, and are now selling at from $40 to $150. The place now has a population of near three hundred of as enterprising, energetic citizens as can be found anywhere, all of whom realize the advantages possessed by their town, and have a well-grounded faith in her future, as is evidenced by the efforts they are making to build up the place, and the additional fact that none are willing to sell out.

The first improvements were made on the town site in 1869, when the railroad company erected a handsome and commodious depot, and a large store building, and two residences were built and a lumber yard opened by Samuel A. Francis—one of the early settlers of Fontenelle—and his brother-in-law, John Waynick, of Chariton, Iowa. Next a grain warehouse was built and successfully operated by L. H. Jones, who was the first station agent of the railroad company, and soon after, A. C. Mansfield opened a store with a large stock of goods, specially adapted to the wants of the country. In 1870, Dr. S. G. Glover, opened a drug store. John Butler built a blacksmith shop, and John A. Unthank, a grain elevator.

In 1872, Nathan Foster, engaged in the lumber business in the new town. E. K. Gilbert opened a shoe shop, and Butler's blacksmith shop was bought by Chris. Hamming, J. C. Blackburn engaged extensively in the sale of hardware and agricultural implements, W. J. Crane became agent for the railroad company, vice Jones, and also engaged in grain buying in company with R. E. Roberts, and G. Hershoff, bought out Hamming's blacksmith shop.

In 1873, David Bender established a grocery store. Silas Masters built the Eagle Hotel, R E. Roberts built a grain warehouse—which afterwards developed into a large elevator—Mr. Bender sold out his grocery and in company with Hayman Chapman went into the dry goods and grocery business on a more extensive scale, a lodge of Odd Fellows and another of the Sons of Temperance were organized, Williams & Curtis opened a paint shop, W. S. Cook a meat market and Henry Osterman a saloon.

During 1874, a blacksmith shop was built by John Hamming and a wagon shop by J. H. Stewart.

In 1875, the Masons organized a lodge, Bender & Chapman having dissolved, Mr. Chapman started in business for himself in the same line, W. Crane resigned his position of station agent, closed out a stock of goods bought of Mr. Chapman, in the following spring, and went into a general insurance, real estate and collecting business. A public school building to cost $5,000 was commenced and is now about completed, Joseph Snyder opened a shoe shop, and Dr. Elwood associated himself in the practice of medicine with Dr. Glover. Thus far this year no material business changes have taken place in the town, though it shows a steady increase of population.

The first marriage in Bell Creek was that of Mr. Joshua G. Benster and Miss Cora Jones, daughter of L. H. Jones, the first birth being that of a son of Mr. Butler whom he named Bertie. Miss Kate Parker taught the first school. The town commands the trade of a splendid section of the country, and is accessible therefrom at all seasons of the year by means of ridge roads which cross but few streams or sloughs. There is no town in the state of equal size from which more grain, cattle and hogs are shipped, for the handling of which first-class facilities have been provided. Last year Mr. Blackburn did a business of $20,000 in hardware, wagons, agricultural implements, etc., while Mansfield and Chapman, the leading merchants, each sold nearly that amount of goods.

Russell Miller's dau. died. I visited her while and preached her funeral [sermon]. He lives in ur called the Indiana settlement. (J. Waller) 1898

RICHLAND PRECINCT.

An Old Time Settlement—How it Got its Name.

The settlement of what is now the southwestern part of Washington county was begun in the summer of 1856. Russel Miller and his three sons-in-law made the first *bona fide* settlement. They all took three hundred and twenty acre claims, agreeably to the Omaha Club law, which became the rule also of the Elkhorn club. Miller took the north half of section 28, and Adams, Lyons, and Dowling, his three sons-in law, took adjoining claims. Miller broke some prairie and they erected two or three houses. Miller bought the claim of one who had preceeded him, and who perhaps did the first breaking and built the first house, in which Mrs. Adams lived and died. When the precinct was formed it was called Richland because Miller refused to have it called by his name and suggested the name of Richland, that being the place in Ohio from which he came.

Henry Wright broke a strip where S. S. Blanchard lives. He sold to Mr. W. E. Purchase, and "held" the claim for him for a while. Purchase brought a saw mill that summer or fall, the third in all the country around. The first was at Fontenelle; Shields', at Elkhorn ferry, on the military road to Fort Kearney, was second, and the one at Irou Bluff's or at West Point made the fourth. A man by the name of Oaks, who merely held the claim without breaking the sod was located just north of L. P. Jenks. Fox, of Fontenelle carried the mail on foot to and from Omaha, forty miles.

Some time that summer (1856) H. R. Benjamin, now of Omaha, C. A. Whitford, and Odillon Whitford took claims in sections 8 and 9. They built a substantial log house, very near where C. A. Whitford's new residence is. It was for years after known as the Indiana House, that being the State from which they came. Silas Masters built a log house on his farm in the fall of 1856.—Dennis, Caleb Winch, and Adam Studt bought claims and occupied them in the fall and winter of 1856-7, Dennis, where A. F. Warner now lives; Winch, at L. P. Jenks' residence, and Studt, where that of F. Benard now is. Theophilus Thompson and R. B. Brown wintered at Thompson's west of Blanchard's, on Walnut creek. Brown's claim was south of Taylor's. Orrin Colby came in the summer of 1856 and put up a small house near his present dwelling, and now has one of the finest farms in the country. McNaughton occupied a little cabin where George T. Taylor's farm house now stands.

In the spring of 1857, a number of settlers came in. Judge J.S. Bowen, now editor of the Blair *Times*, his son Will R. Bowen, now of Omaha, and Dr. Heaton took claims in sections 13 and 14. Joseph Levi and Hiram Johnson also took claims in section 23, and with their mothers and sisters resided on Hiram's claim. Azariah Masters, sr., father of Silas and Azariah, put up a substantial log house where Munson Downs now lives. McVickar also came and joined McNaughton in sections 15 and 22, now George T. Taylor's farm. In the summer of 1857 Mrs. Adams, daughter of Russell Miller, died, leaving a husband and two children, who soon after returned to Ohio. Nathaniel Brewster, early in the summer of 1857, put up a house on the hill just north of the present depot at Kennard. The house was burned down some years after.

In 1858 David Bender came and built a good house in section nine. His son-in-law, Amos Shick, came about the same time, and was engaged at the saw mill. He afterwards took and improved land in section three. John Hilton came in the summer of 1858, and lived in the Thompson house, (west of Blanchard's.) He died there not long after, and, to add to the affliction of the widow, the house with its contents was burned up within a few weeks after his death. Dr. Benjamin sold out to Simon Hammer and his brother-in-law, Hadley, and they divided the tract in section nine between them. John B. Ultz and Mrs. Ultz, Mrs. Ultz being the mother of Mr. Hammer and Mrs. Hadley, came with them. Hadley, some years after, went to Missouri. Mr. Hammer and the old Mr. Ultz are living in Bell Creek. Milo F. Young held the land now owned by George C. Pemberton for a year or so, next north of Benjamin's. John Mattes, now residing on the old Miller claim, lived north of Silas Masters on part of Wm. Hilginkamp's land. John A. Unthank and Azariah Masters came in the fall of 1858. Peter S. Reed and T. C. Powers came in the same season, and took claims in section twenty-four. Reed was an energetic man, and, having seen service in the Mexican war, became captain of company A, 2nd Nebraska, which was formed in 1862 chiefly of citizens of Fontenelle, Richland and Fort Calhoun. Richland furnished eighteen of the company. Evelin Purchase, A. J. Warner, the Tomlinson brothers, and some others came early, but did not make definite location until after several years had elapsed.

The breaking out of the Pike's Peak gold fever, and the drainage of population from that cause and from the war that soon followed, removed permanently, or temporarily, a number of settlers, and the return of some of them with the settlers of later date need not here be chronicled. The precinct has long been noted for its beautiful farms and handsome and extensive groves—its first settlers having set an excellent example to those who followed them, in the way of tree planting.

THE WASHINGTON COUNTY OF TO-DAY.

ITS CONDITION, RESOURCES AND ADVANTAGES BRIEFLY STATED.

In this centennial year of national independence, throughout the length and breadth of our magnificent land, there is no section of country which offers to the emigrant fairer prospects or more certain and speedy returns for the outlay of capital or labor, than does Washington county. The Missouri river on the east and the Elkhorn on the west, form a verdant fringe to the immense pattern in progress of weaving across which the plow speeds back and forth like a shuttle, throwing up in relief the outlines of towns and future cities as figures on its surface, while the general plan is filled in waving corn, golden wheat, nodding woodlands and running streams. Wonderful, wonderful have been the changes wrought in the condition of the county during the time of which this history speaks. But who can picture the still more wonderful transformations which this county will have undergone when two more decades have come and passed, and the year 1896 dawns upon us?

At the present time, there are within the county, forty-six school districts, each provided with a good house for school purposes, varying in cost from $500 to $15,000. These houses will compare very favorably in appearance and accommodations with the school houses in many of the older states, and are well supplied with maps, charts and globes—in fact all the necessary apparatus for teaching upon the most approved modern principles. There are annually employed in the county seventy-four teachers, male and female, and the total number of children of school age is 2,323. The amount of wages paid to teachers for the fiscal year ending July 1st, 1876, was $11,626.95, and the total value of school property in the county at the present time, is $49,970.

Religious interests in the county are not neglected, there being now within her boundaries twenty-thre organized church societies, representing thirteen denominations, many of which have elegant church edifices. There are at this time in the county, four Masonic, several Temperance, and three Odd Fellow organizations, while the order of the patrons of husbandry has a large membership. The Grange movement started in Washington county early in the fall of 1873, when Washington Grange

No. 130 was organized at or near Fontenelle, and so rapid was its progress that in the spring of 1874 there were seventeen Granges in the county, with an average membership of over thirty, making a total of over five hundred members of the order of which about four hundred were voters and one hundred ladies and young men under age. The order was very prosperous during the year 1874, and many new members were added to the several Granges, and on the 4th of July of that year, the argest celebration ever had in the country, was had under their auspices in a grove at the head of New York Creek.

Early in 1874 a county council of the order was organized but for want of established rules for its government did not prove a success and a Pomona Grange took its place in March, 1876, being the second Pomona Grange organized in the State. This Grange is located at Blair the county seat and is composed of representatives from each Grange in the county It is expected that much good for the order will result from this organization,

Washington county contains 400 square miles, or about 256,000 acres of land; of which about one-eighth are river or creek bottoms. The rest of the country is rolling prairie, as smooth and even as is compatible with a well watered country and good drainage. The bottoms are dark alluvial, chiefly vegetable mould, 4 to 20 feet deep. The uplands which are from fifty to one hundred and fifty feet above the bottoms, are a dark loam, rich in vegetable matter, from one to six feet deep, upon a subsoil of a light marly loam from twenty to thirty feet in depth, resting on clay. The soil is coarse quality, able to resist continued drouth, and is never soggy from excess of moisture.

The prairies are covered with a heavy coat of blue-joint grass, affording rich pasturage and nutritious hay. Tame grasses are not needed, though they have been successfully raised. Timothy, red-top, white and red clover, Hungarian and other grasses do well. Kentucky blue-grass flourishes, and where started takes posession of the prairie. Every species of grain and roots grown in older settlements is raised here with ease and profit. There are now in cultivation over 180,000 acres in the county. Many farms have superior improvements. There are a number of good orchards growing, as fine fruits as those of any State to the East or West. The average crops for the last five years have been, of wheat 15 bushels to the acre, corn 50 to 75 bushels, oats the same, barley 30, buckwheat 30, potatoes 60 to 100, hay 1½ to 3 tons.

Several large mills have been erected upon the Elkhorn, and its abundant water power will soon be converted into more general use. Quite a number of smaller streams water the county, some of which have good mill sites. Among these are Fish, Long, New York, Stewart, North, South, Bell, Turkey, Deer, Moore, Little Bell, Brown, Walnut and other streams, besides the Papillion with its branches, which drains a large part of the county. Lumber grows in large bodies along the Missouri and Elkhorn rivers, and upon a number of the smaller streams; and is chiefly owned by actual settlers, and can be bought for from $10 to

$30 per acre. The timber of the bottom lands is principally cottonwood, interspersed with ash, elm and other hard wood. That of the valley hills and on smaller streams, is chiefly oak, walnut and hickory.

The county contains nearly 7,000 inhabitants. There are 20,000 acres of land in the county belonging to the Union Pacific and the Sioux City and Pacific railroads, for sale on from five to ten years time, with six and ten per cent. interest, payable two years after date of contract, at from six to twelve dollars per acre, and are some of the best lands in the county. The rate of taxation is from two and one-half to three and one-half per cent. The assessed valuation is far below market value.

ACKNOWLEDGMENTS.

In closing this sketch, the writer desires to return thanks to John S. Bowen, E. H. Clark, Col. and Mrs. Wm. Kline, E. S. Gaylord, Perry Selden, Judge Jesse T. Davis, E. C. Jackson, J. H. Hungate, Alex. Reed, A. Castetter, E. M. Denny, W. J. Crane, J. A. Unthank, Harlow J. Carpenter, William A. Bell and J. C. Blackburn, for assistance rendered in collecting material therefor. It may be that some will be disappointed because this is not a volume of several hundred pages, "bound in calf," with gilt edges and a picture of a train of cars chasing a herd of buffaloes on each cover. The only reason why I do not get up such a publication, is because it wouldn't pay. That task I cheerfully leave to that much-referred-to-individual—the Future Historian, who is popularly supposed to be a man of leisurely, methodical habits, with an abundance of time and funds, and an unquenchable desire for glory.

ADVERTISEMENTS.

J. C. BLACKBURN,

DEALER IN AND AGENT FOR

Buckeye Reapers and Mowers

Marsh Harvesters, Wm. A. Wood's Mowers

Buckeye Drills, Buckeye and Fountain City Seeders, Spic's Harrows, Burtrand & Same's Riding, Eureka Riding and Walking, Davenport Walking and Weir Walking Corn Plows; Furst & Bradley and Hapgood 16-inch Sulky Plows; 14 and 16-inch wood and iron beam Walking Plows, Prairie King Breakers, Brown and Keystone Corn Planters, Wagons, Hardware, Stoves and Tinware.

BELL CREEK, WASHINGTON CO., NEB.

KENNY & STEWART'S

HARDWARE HOUSE,

(One of the Oldest in the County)

Blair, Nebraska.

STOVES and a full assortment of TINWARE.

Full and Fine assortment of Table and Pocket Cutlery. Iron, Nails, Wagon Woods, Blacksmith's Stock, Guns, Powder, Shot and Caps. A full assortment of

House Furnishing Goods.

Hay Forks, Hoes, Shovels, Spades and Scrapers, Furst & Bradley Gang Plows. Furst & Bradley 16-inch Sulky Plow, Furst & Bradley Stirring Plows. Furst & Bradley Breaking Plows, Furst & Bradley Combined Cultivators, Furst & Bradley Sulky Rake. Scotch & Friedman Harrow. Rope of all Sizes. The finest assortment of SHELF HARDWARE north of Omaha.

ADVERTISEMENTS.

W. J. CRANE,
Notary Public,
Insurance, Collecting & Real Estate Agent.
AGENT FOR TOWN LOTS.

Taxes Paid on non-Resident Lands. Information given as to Value, Location, &c. Abstract of Titles sent on application. Correspondence solicited.

Address, **W. H. CRANE**,
Real Estate Agent, BELL CREEK, NEB.

Established August, 1873.

HAYMAN CHAPMAN,
DEALER IN
DRY GOODS!

Queensware, Groceries,
READY-MADE CLOTHING, HATS, CAPS, BOOTS & SHOES.
Highest Market Price Paid for Country Produce.

BELL CREEK, - NEBRASKA.

NATHAN FOSTER, Jr.,
DEALER IN
Lumber, Lath, Shingles, Sash, Doors, Blinds
LOUISVILLE CEMENT,
Lime, Hair, Stucco, Sheathing and Felt,
BELL CREEK, WASHINGTON CO., NEB.

Staple and Fancy Dry Goods
JUST RECEIVED BY
HALLER BROTHERS,

Opposite Castetter's Bank,   Blair, Neb.

ADVERTISEMENTS.

THE NEW FLOURING MILL
AT BLAIR

Is now open for business, and farmers can be accommodated with

Grist or Exchange Work.

They keep constantly on hand

FLOUR, BRAN, SHORTS, MIXED FEED, MEAL, &c.,

Which is for Sale or Exchange on reasonable terms.

ALEX. REED,
Real Estate Agent
AND
NOTARY PUBLIC.

Agent for the Purchase and Sale of Real Estate and Payment of Taxes. I HAVE FOR SALE IMPROVED AND UNIMPROVED LANDS in all parts of the County. Keep a complete Abstract of Titles to all Real Estate in Washington County. **Blair, Neb.**

F. H. MATTHIESEN.   C. C. LOGAN.

MATTHIESEN & LOGAN,
BLAIR, NEBRASKA,

Have received their new stock of

CLOTHING!

TIES, COLLARS,
STAPLE AND FANCY DRY GOODS, &C.

Prices Lower than Ever Before.

O. V. PALMER & CO.,
DEXTER'S BLOCK.
Blair, Neb.,
HAVE

BOOTS, SHOES,
GROCERIES, QUEENSWARE, HATS AND CAPS,
DRY GOODS.

Also a full line of Staple and Fancy Articles at prices which defy competition.

ADVERTISEMENTS.

C. C. CROWELL.   A. P. HOWES.

C. C. CROWELL & CO.,

DEALERS IN

Lumber, Sash, Doors, Lath,

COAL, LIME, CEMENT, &c.

Special Rates on Large Bills.

OFFICE AND YARD—Opposite R. R. Depot.

BLAIR, - - - - - NEBRASKA.

The New Regulator,

At Rosa's Old Corner **BLAIR, NEB.**, Is the Place to buy

DRY GOODS

AND

GROCERIES

At the Lowest Cash Figures.

ROSA & FISHER.

HALLER & LANE,

Wholesale and Retail Dealers in

DRUGS, MEDICINES

OILS, PAINTS, FANCY GOODS,

Dye Stuff, Putty, Brushes and Glass. The Purest and Oldest BOURBON WHISKY, and Imported and Native Wines and Brandies for Medical Purposes, CIGARS, Toilet Articles, Trusses, Syringes, &c. Physicians' Prescriptions a specialty. Very low cash prices.

Washington street, one door East of A. Castetter's Bank, **BLAIR, NEB.**

ADVERTISEMENTS.

E. M. DENNY,

DEALER IN

MARSH HARVERTER,

Agricultural Implements, Diamond Mowers, Improved Rakes, Davenport Stirring and Breaking Plows, Riding and Walking Cultivators, MARSH SULKY CULTIVATORS, CORN SHELLERS, HARRISON WAGONS, PUMPS, ETC., ETC.,

Washington Street, Blair.

ADOLPH ALBRECHT,

GROCER

AND DEALER IN

CIGARS, TOBACCO, DRY GOODS, BOOTS, & SHOES,

Patent Medicines,

Crockery Hardware, Tinware, Etc.,

FORT CALHOUN, NEB.

HERMAN BROS.,

Blair, Nebraska,

DEALER IN

Dry Goods, Groceries, Provisions,

CLOTHING, BOOTS, SHOES, HATS, CAPS, &c.

Also in CATTTLE, HOGS and CORN. The oldest firm in Blair, where they have been constantly engaged in business since the organization of the town.

ALONZO PERKINS,

Loan, Collection and Real Estate Agent,

BLAIR, NEBRASKA,

Will pay the highest market price for School Bonds. Money Loaned on Improved Farms in sums to suit.

ADVERTISEMENTS.

ELAM CLARK & SON,

PROPRIETORS

Calhoun and Waterloo

FLOURING MILLS

ALSO OF

Grain Elevators at Blair and Herman.

GENERAL DEALERS IN FLOUR, FEED AND GRAIN.

Main Office and Store Rooms at

OMAHA, NEBRASKA.

THE TIMES,

PUBLISHED AT

Blair, Nebraska, Every Thursday,

AT $2.00 PER ANNUM.

JOHN S. BOWEN, Editor and Proprietor.

JOHN T. BELL,   HOMER STULL,
Official Reporter Third District.   U. S. Examiner in Chancery.

BELL & STULL,

Short Hand Writers and Notaries,

OMAHA, NEB., will visit any portion of the state and Report Conventions, Speeches, Lectures, Court Proceedings, etc.

THE PILOT,

The Official Paper of Washington Co. is Published

EVERY THURSDAY MORNING AT BLAIR, NEBRASKA.

L. F. HILTON, Editor.

TERMS—Two Dollars per Year.

www.ingramcontent.com/pod-product-compliance
Lightning Source LLC
Chambersburg PA
CBHW022151090426
42742CB00010B/1474